Wisdom Found

STORIES OF WOMEN TRANSFIGURED BY FAITH

Edited by

LINDSAY HARDIN FREEMAN

FORWARD MOVEMENT

Cincinnati, Ohio

FORWARD MOVEMENT, an official, non-profit agency of the Episcopal Church, is sustained through sales and tax-free contributions from our readers.

Book design: Albonetti Design
Carole Miller

FORWARD MOVEMENT
412 Sycamore Street, Cincinnati, Ohio 45202-4195
800-543-1813
www.forwardmovement.org

Contents

Preface

Lindsay Hardin Freeman, editor

Some two thousand years ago, a small group of women took to the cold streets of Jerusalem before dawn. Deep in grief, they mourned the violent death of their friend Jesus. They had believed in him; they knew him as companion and leader; yet he was gone. Images of his gruesome death flashed in their minds.

Thankfully, there was work to do: his body to prepare and anoint, and goodbyes to be said. Hands filled with linens and hearts filled with loss, they walked together, not saying much, not having to say much. Memories of better days were ingrained, days when hope and joy were intertwined like Ruth and Naomi, Mary and Martha, Deborah and Jael.

The women would not abandon the task before them; they would get through it because they had each other. On that morning when all was dark, they did what they had done so many other times: they stood together.

And that is the way it has always been with women. We grieve together, we laugh, we hold each other up. In each other's company, valleys are raised up and mountains are made low.

When that connection is based on faith—when the Holy Spirit dances in the middle like a blazing fire inviting, warming, and beckoning—the bond is even tighter, the foundation even stronger.

Written from inside that circle of faith, this book is filled with nearly a hundred contributions: poems, stories, and meditations, all written by women, lay and clergy alike.

Some of the authors, like Barbara Cawthorne Crafton and Rosemary Radford Ruether, are well-known. Others have never written professionally. But their journeys—whether about illness or courage or heartbreak—have much common ground, much common faith.

So join us, come close around the fire. Like those women at the tomb so many years ago, you might be surprised, or you might laugh or shed a tear. Whatever your response, your presence is most welcome here—in God's sacred circle.

With Gratitude

A deep thank you goes to all who helped this book come together, especially those forty women who answered the call to write. Passionate beliefs were expressed; experiences were raised up; vulnerabilities were shared; and faith shone through. Women have always drawn strength from each other and given freely of their wisdom. The authors in this book carry on that great tradition.

Thank you also to my husband Leonard for his never-ending support, faith, and significant contributions on many levels. Poetry editor David Freeman assessed rhyme and meter and verse, and Catholic lay worker Theresa Zlotkowski suggested some of the classic quotations.

Finally, a word about Forward Movement, written from an outside perspective, as one who was asked to edit this book. Forward Movement celebrated its 75th anniversary in 2010. Over those seventy-five years, in addition to the daily devotional *Forward Day by Day,* some three thousand publications have been produced, all of which have enriched and deepened the life of both Episcopalians and non-Episcopalians. *Forward Day by Day,* the flagship publication, is read across the globe every day, with 350,000 print copies distributed each quarter.

We are all in debt to Forward Movement, both to its retiring editor and director, the Rev. Dr. Richard H. Schmidt, and to the staff for their invaluable support, especially Janet Buening and Carole Miller, who contributed much energy and spirit to this book. May God continue to bless all those who share in the ministry of writing, authors and publishers alike. And thanks be that the *Word*—with a capital "W"—continues to make it all worthwhile. —**LHF**

CHAPTER 1

Finding a Balance

THE GOD OF MULTITASKING

BARBARA CAWTHORNE CRAFTON

Ironing while helping with homework. Cooking while helping with homework. Folding clothes while listening to the news while cuddling a toddler who's unfolding the clothes. Writing while waiting for a plane. Practicing spelling words with a fourth grader while driving.

Women become so accustomed to doing several things at once that some of us feel lazy if we catch ourselves doing only one. We've been on duty for so long that we don't even remember what it was like not to have work to do. We're not even sure we want to find out—who would I be without all my jobs? Mightn't I just disappear?

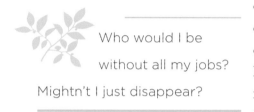

Who would I be without all my jobs? Mightn't I just disappear?

We mustn't multitask, the psychologist on the radio warns us. Try to do several things at once, he says, and you end up not doing any of them very well. Hmm—bet anything he's always had someone in the background of his life making sure he didn't have to do more than one thing at a time.

Maybe he's right, and good for him, I say—but many women just don't have the luxury of such single-mindedness.

Many gods and goddesses of the Hindu faith have multiple arms, an expression of their potency in a variety of simultaneous activities. I've always been drawn to them—who hasn't wished for an extra pair of hands now and then? But Jesus had just two hands, as you and I do. He was limited, as we are. In over his head, sometimes—just like me. Desperately needing some downtime, like me. More than once, we see him withdrawing in search of uninterrupted quiet—and then we see people finding him, so they can interrupt him. I think I can hear him thinking: *Ah, well. It was nice while it lasted.*

It's so good when we can grab some single-minded time. It's like really feeling your bare toes in green grass—you're so in touch with exactly who and where you are. But soon it's time to put your shoes back on and get back to work. It was nice while it lasted.

MARY ON THE MOVE
NANCY HOPKINS-GREENE

One year for Mother's Day, my children gave me a plaster statue of the Virgin Mary. About a foot tall, it is a bust of Mary, eyes lowered, oversized hands open. It portrays Mary in her moment of acceptance, when she said to God's messenger, "Here I am, the servant of the Lord; let it be with me according to your word." Delighted, I placed the figure in a prominent place in our living room.

> Hurried, stressed Mommy needed some comforting that morning.

But then, a few weeks later, the statue—*she*—began to roam. The first time she disappeared, I found her in the doll cradle in my four-year-old daughter Sarah's room. Mary's head was wrapped in a pink blanket. I told Sarah that I was happy she liked it, but that Mary was not a toy. Back in the living room the statue went.

The next time Mary went on the move, she was taking a ride in a Little Tikes® pink and white plastic stroller. I mused over the fact that Mary—like many mothers—couldn't seem to stay still.

One morning, exasperated, with two children refusing to get dressed and all of us running late, I stormed into Sarah's room to see what was taking her so long. Looking up at me, she went and picked up the statue of Mary which had found its way back into the cradle. Then she held her. Patted her head. Cradled her. Rocked her. I realized at that moment that she was comforting and cradling me. Hurried, stressed Mommy needed some comforting that morning. It was the crèche in reverse, the child cradling the mother.

Mary finally found a permanent home on Sarah's bedside table. Sometimes she wore necklaces and hats. She spent an occasional night in the cradle.

Like so many women, I often find myself feeling overwhelmed and stressed. Mary-on-the-move reminds me of my need to accept, to slow down, to be comforted—to open my hands and let go. Mary's prayer is mine, too: *Let it be with me according to your word.*

STEP ASIDE, PROVERBS 31 WOMAN
CORALIE VOCE HAMBLETON

She rises while it is still night
and provides food for her household…
she considers a field and buys it;
with the fruit of her hands she plants a vineyard.
—PROVERBS 31:15–16

The saying goes that my age group is part of "the sandwich generation," the one juggling to care for children and elders at the same time.

This year I feel like someone has taken several bites out of my slice of bologna, and forgotten the mayo as well.

There doesn't seem to be enough of me to get done what I believe I'm supposed to be doing. My mother is in a nursing home. I thought when she was placed in twenty-four-hour care that her demands on my time would lessen because her needs would be met and I'd be able to just enjoy visiting with her, rather than accomplishing the ninety things she'd have me do each time I went to visit her at home.

Wrong.

Now there's a gazillion other things she needs me to do. I'm in charge of sorting and cleaning her house out; did I mention that my mother *saved* everything? Yep, every statement, receipt, pictures made by growing little hands, letters… My grandmother saved everything too. My mom was born in that house. Sometimes I think I'm going to *die* in that house!

My remaining son at home has special needs; my two older sons, one with my two cherished grandsons, like to have me visit now and then. I work nights part-time, I'm a vocational deacon at my church, and my husband would like to see me sometime. We're well acquainted with the "two ships passing in the dark" scenario.

I feel like a juggler with so many balls flying through the air that something's going to get dropped—and then what? And sometimes I just need some downtime to read or quilt, which helps center me (doesn't feel like much of that either).

Daily devotions? The sitting in a special quiet spot for twenty minutes each day is a pipe dream, and I've come to better understand the "pray without ceasing" part. You know, on the run. But I recognize that this crazy "There's not enough of me to go around" time in my life will pass. I can only do the best I can, with what I can, which isn't perfection, believe me.

> I feel like a juggler with so many balls flying through the air that something's going to get dropped—and then what?

Sadly, Mom will be gone soon. The kids will grow. The house I cleaned today will be dirty tomorrow. There will never really be enough of me to go around, anyway, because God created me to be a "get 'er done" kind of woman.

So step aside, Proverbs 31 Woman, and Lord, will you please pass the mayo?

She girds herself with strength, and makes her arms strong.
She perceives that her merchandise is profitable.
Her lamp does not go out at night.
She puts her hands to the distaff, and her hands hold the spindle.
She opens her hand to the poor, and reaches out her hands to the needy.
She looks well to the ways of her household, and does not eat the bread of the idleness.
—PROVERBS 31:17-20,27

STOPPING THE WORLD

LEE KRUG

Women on the Verge of a Nervous Breakdown is the title of a Broadway play and a movie.

And in that script, when a woman said, "What I need is a wife," it was no joke. Back in the time when men went to work and their wives took care of the home and children, women often worked more hours than men. Today most wives also work outside the home and may be left with no time for reflecting, praying, or dancing.

Remember, God rested—for an entire day of a working week. Try this: Go into your bedroom, close the door, and sit or lie down for twenty minutes. Let your body speak to you. God has given you a female body, whose voice is different from a male's. Your body's inner voice may bring you a message from God. You might hear the words of a hymn:

> *Peace before me,*
> *Peace behind me,*
> *Peace under my feet,*
> *Peace within me,*
> *Peace over me,*
> *Let all around me be peace.*

If you've been running as fast as you can, set aside time to slow down. Perhaps you will not "get it all done," whatever "it" is. Life is chaotic and overwhelming unless you purposefully separate yourself and step into a place of quiet, a sacred space where your soul may rest and be reassured.

When you step off the path for a brief period, consider that God does not talk to us about winning a marathon, but about a meaningful journey.

I LIGHT A CANDLE
CATHY H. GEORGE

Your word is a lantern to my feet and a light upon my path.
—PSALM 119:105

Strike a match, and out of thin air a candle is lit. Something unseen takes its place in the world of what is seen. The world beneath and behind the white birch against blue sky, the smell of fresh ground coffee, the red wagon on the sidewalk making its presence seen and felt in heat and light. Lighting a candle brings to mind what is unseen, hidden, eternal. We are not all there is.

I light a candle to find God in ordinary places. I strike a match and touch it to the wick and hold it there, and without exertion the candle burns. *I am here,* it says to me. *I was always here, but now you can see that I am here.* I light a candle when I begin to pray because I need to create a place for God to be with me in time and space, in earthly life. I see God in the lilac trees exploding with lavender color and a fragrance that is bliss and in my child's motoring legs running from the swing set. I feel God in the wind on my cheek. I taste God in fresh-baked rhubarb crisp—the fruit picked from the garden, washed and chopped—still warm, with melting ice cream.

God is in all these things. I light a candle to bring the Divine into this place. I stop, and plan to do nothing else. To be all for God. To come and rest before the throne and say *I need, I love, I sin, I am sorry, I smile, I am.* To be in eternity, the world where I came from, the world where I will go, to gaze across at the other shore, I light a candle. This solitary place opens out to the whole world. The thin membrane that separates this world from the deeper one is, for a brief time, burned through when the match strikes, the flame ignites, and a wick burns.

> I light a candle when I begin to pray because I need to create a place for God to be with me...

THE PROMISE OF SILENCE
JOY HUNTER

Silence…it is utterly silent. Well, actually the washer and dryer are both rumbling and now this computer is making its whirring sounds. But there are no people sounds. My husband and eldest son have left on a mission trip and my youngest passed on an evening with me for an overnight with a friend.

At first I thought, *A night on my own! I'll celebrate…invite girlfriends over; go shopping; go to the movies; go…*

And then the idea hit: *What if I just spent time with someone I never get time alone with—myself?*

Our lives are frantically frenetic. I'm like a musical jewelry box that's wound too tight to make music.

As I tidied up the kitchen I caught a glimpse of a vase my younger brother made when he was a potter. It's beautiful. Its browns and grays and blacks swirl together. Its smooth, touchable surface almost made me cry.

That took time to make, I thought. It wasn't squeezed between folding

I'm like a musical jewelry box that's wound too tight to make music.

laundry and *American Idol,* between picking up kids and cooking dinner. No. He had to stop. He had to go to his studio, be alone with the clay, and for that time at least, let go of his worries to create.

I wonder if that's what God had in mind when he commanded a Sabbath.

Yes, my musical jewelry box has been wound too tight, but right now—for just this moment, it is winding down. The music is sweeter, going slower and slower and slower…

And for a few moments, at least for tonight, I will let it stop, and enjoy the silence.

SLOWING DOWN
NANCY HOPKINS-GREENE

Like many women, I am a pro at multitasking as I manage a family, a household, and two jobs. Competency and efficiency are gifts from God, but there are times when I miss God's presence as I speed through life. Words from the prayer "Slow Me Down, Lord," by Wilferd A. Peterson speak to me:

Remind me each day
That the race is not always to the swift;
That there is more to life
Than increasing its speed.

Let me look upward
Into the branches of the towering oak
And know that it grew great and strong
Because it grew slowly and well.

This past summer, two new experiences taught me to slow down. First, I put up a clothesline. I'm guessing that some old neighborhood association by-laws forbid it. But no one dared to confront me. Second, I finally installed a rain barrel under one of our downspouts.

Both of these probably sound like attempts at being "green," which they are, of course. But I've learned other lessons, too. Instead of throwing a load of laundry from the washer into the dryer in less than a minute, I have to handle each piece of clothing, hang it on the line, and later take each piece down. As for the rain barrel, it fills quickly after a big rainstorm. But it takes time to fill the watering can over and over and to lug it around my garden to water the plants.

These forced slowdowns in my days have become contemplative moments. They are times when I live in the present moment, when I am grateful—not only for the breeze that dries my clothes and the rain that waters my garden—but for all of my life.

CHANGE AND ROUTINE
ERIN MARTINEAU

I had to get to a quiet place to be able to breathe again, to feel the spirit move. City life, cable news, gym membership, fancy shoes: I was running on an adrenaline high that lasted years. But the gloss wore off, and I felt it—I was tired in my bones.

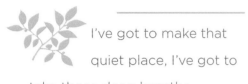

I've got to make that quiet place, I've got to take those deep breaths.

Every weekend I took the train out of the concrete, past the spendy towns, past the reservoirs, to a little farm. And I knelt in the dirt, astounded by life. Dark, fluffy dirt teeming with creatures, and the sprouting of seeds climbing to the light. I wanted to be such a seed, to burst open, to flourish. The spirit was there, with me, as I dug, planted, watered, tended.

In the fields, among the crops, the gospel rang in my ears: *Follow me.* I had just spent most of a decade getting a degree, neatly arranging all the details of a career. Could I just turn and walk away? Could I release that ambition, that investment, those years? Could I "let the dead bury their own dead"? (Matthew 8:22).

I took the big leap, moved to the farm. And when I am on my hands and knees in the garden, the birdsong rings out over the cars rushing by. The rhythm of planting creates space in my brain. I breathe deep. I am in the flow.

Unless I'm not.

A year later: I find, to my disappointment, that I still worry, that I get frustrated, conflicted. Turns out that it takes work to stay in the flow, to be open to the spirit. I've got to make that quiet place, I've got to take those deep breaths. I've got to let go repeatedly. Transformation, it seems, is an everyday project.

MUTTON DRESSED LIKE LAMB
SARAH BRYAN MILLER

"Mutton dressed like lamb," my mother would mutter on seeing an older woman wearing clothing and other stylistic choices intended for a much younger person. It's an expression that comes to my mind frequently these days, as our cultural obsession with youth, or at least the appearance of youth, grows completely out of hand.

Now, it may be that "fifty is the new forty" (I certainly hope so), as improved medical care and lifestyles keep us healthier for longer than in earlier generations. But neither fifty nor forty is the new twenty, and we look foolish if we try to pretend it is. While no one wants to look older than she is, clothes and hairstyles, makeup and plastic surgery may sometimes blur but cannot really erase the years.

There's an art to aging gracefully, and I suspect that at least some of it involves accepting who and what we are at any given time. I would not exchange the experiences I've had or the knowledge I've acquired for another shot at youth.

Each age has its own challenges and difficulties that seem immense at the time: the small but very real woes of children who are just learning to deal with the world; the angst and awkwardness of adolescence; the young adult finding a way; the every-which-way responsibilities of middle age; the fears and loneliness that often accompany old age.

I would not exchange the experiences I've had or the knowledge I've acquired for another shot at youth.

There's an element of grace in knowing where we are in the continuum, and in accepting the challenges as they come in their seasons. Faith helps in this. Our own challenges may differ in material ways from those faced by our mothers and grandmothers, but the essential outlines are as timeless as God's Creation itself.

MORNING COFFEE
NANCY HOPKINS-GREENE

when the wind blows just right

when I am open to what is
  instead of focused on what needs to be done

when I am listening
  instead of talking

when I am sipping my morning coffee
  instead of gulping it down

when I am softly awaiting a day
  instead of rigidly planning it

when the windows are open and my heart is open too
  I hear the bells of Guardian Angels Church

CHAPTER 2

Work and Play

TO FAIL OR NOT TO FAIL
CYNTHIA CARUSO

It was one of the hardest years of my middle-class life, teaching fifth grade on the Zuni reservation. My principal assured me that it would be far better than the semester I had just experienced at the high school, where I was called names I can't repeat.

She was right, but it was still very difficult. I was not of them, and these ten-year-olds seemed to delight in making me feel "Other."

"Have you ever seen a shooting star?" I asked after reading that image in a poem.

"We're not allowed to look at them," shouted back Sylvia, a defiant girl. "It is not part of our culture."

If a girl was crying at her desk and I took her into the hall to hear that her father was in jail, or her grandmother was dying, I would ask, "May I give you a hug?"

"No!" she would say.

When I asked them if they were enjoying Hogwarts as we got deep into the first of the six Harry Potter books that we read together, the answer was, again, "No."

It is hard to convey how difficult it is to work day after day, failing. It kills one's spirit a few cells at a time.

So I was glad to leave in May, thankful that I would not be "Other" any longer. I moved to Austin, enrolled in seminary, and deliberately worked at defusing my anger and sadness to return to spiritual health.

Then, one hot July afternoon as I walked to the store, my phone buzzed. It was a text from Sylvia, "What's up?"

She and I text weekly now. Danielle also texts me, and I have written to, and heard from, seventeen of my twenty-three students. I pray for them all, daily commending them to God, in alphabetical order by name: Christy, Keera, Keisha… Amen.

BUTTERFLY
CAROL McCREA

Age three, at a church bake sale, I pounded a piano.
Embarrassed, my mother whispered, "This is God's house."
I pounded louder. Horrified, she grabbed me. "Why are you
doing this?"

"Because God'll come down mad, and I'll get to see him." There began my
struggling with unseeable things, my first stage of spiritual development.

More painful was the second stage which involved disbelief, disappointment,
or disgust. "Sophisticated" writers/speakers/teachers say it is neither cool
nor scientific to believe. Worse, people are harmed and abused by religion—
physically, emotionally, and spiritually. Larceny, power, torture, and murder are
perpetrated in the name of gods.

As a college professor, I was agnostic. Even though I had everything I wanted,
I was not happy. God took mercy on me and humorously engineered
my third stage of spiritual development: rebirth. Imagine a feminist,
sophisticated college professor looking down arrogantly at a submissive
evangelical wife. God's grace enabled me to ask her why she was happy, and she
told me her conversion story. Then one day, in deepest misery, I asked Jesus to
come into my life, and he did.

Jesus kept pushing me into a fourth stage of spiritual development: giving up
false gods of alcohol, tobacco, food, caffeine, and work.

My last stage of development will be death and emergence into new,
unknown life. It's not that God will keep me out of heaven. It's that if I don't
develop, I'll be like a caterpillar, dead in my chrysalis, heartbreaking to God and
Savior, who wants each of us to fly.

Once I had said sneeringly to my mother that old people were pious because
they were scared and closer to death. Now I suspect that they had not merely
"withered into the truth" as Yeats wrote, but had developed into it.

RE: DOMESTICITY

SARAH BRYAN MILLER

No one has ever accused me of being a domestic goddess. On the Mary/Martha scale of household aptitude, I'm at least 98 percent Mary.

I know most of the basics. I can cook several things, some without cutting myself or burning something. I can sew on a button, and my daughters survived their childhoods intact. But it must be faced: when it comes to practicing the traditional womanly arts, I'm pretty much a dud.

I blame my ineptitude on the fact that my talents and interests lie in other directions. But I've become more of a small-scale cook lately, driven by equal parts of desire and necessity.

When it comes to practicing the traditional womanly arts, I'm pretty much a dud.

I recently baked an angel food cake from a box. That's easy enough, and you wouldn't have to be Martha Stewart to sneer at that. But I had to remember to buy the mix, and heat the oven, and find the angel food cake pan and scrub it because somebody put it away with goop baked onto the inside, and figure out my mother's fancy KitchenAid mixer and use it, and pour the sticky freshly mixed goop into the pan without getting it all over everything, and bake it for just the right amount of time, and find something on which to place it to cool, and clean up after myself.

For me, the anti-Martha Stewart, it was an accomplishment. The next time I did it, the prep took under five minutes.

I have a theory that we have to keep pushing ourselves or lose our momentum, to stretch in ways we might not have foreseen, to develop new interests and new ways to see the world. I'll keep plugging away in the kitchen and keep learning and improving and trying new things. I'll never be a Martha, but I don't have to be.

FOLDING CLOTHES
ANNE O. WEATHERHOLT

I pray when I fold the laundry. It is one of those chores that never ends as day by day, week by week, the dirty clothes descend to the depths of my basement, are swished with water and soap, spun and dried, and clustered in the baskets. Then they ascend to the bedroom where each garment is taken forth, shaken, and folded to be placed again into waiting drawers that open to the light then close as eyelids into sleep.

Some say that after a loved one dies the bereft seek refuge in their closets, inhaling the secretive, unique smell that lingers on cloth worn pressed next to flesh. I know that, as I lift each garment, I image its shape and presence close to those I love as I sort and stack. Even the towels and sheets have a place in this benediction because I know they will lie beneath or upon prone limbs, or lavish their presence around shoulders or heads.

I silently bless each garment, thus blessing those who will draw this cloth close to them, endowing it with their own scent, the oils of incarnation wiped upon feet and limbs and face, while my own cup runs over with thanksgiving.

Maybe I'm not making big changes in the world,
but if I have somehow helped or encouraged
somebody along the journey,
then I've done what I'm called to do.
SISTER THEA BOWMAN,
AFRICAN AMERICAN FRANCISCAN
(1937–1990)

WHISTLING

LAUREN R. STANLEY

I love to whistle. I whistle in the car and out walking, at work and at play, in home and even in church. It is as much a part of me as my name.

Shortly after I arrived in Southern Sudan, I was whistling as I walked to work. I did not understand the strange looks people on the streets gave me. I thought they were because I was a white woman, an American, a female priest, in a place with no other white people, no other Americans, and very few female priests.

Once settled at work, I began to whistle again. This time, a colleague was with me.

"What are you doing?" he asked, startled and drawing back.

"Working," I replied.

"No. Why are you whistling?" he demanded.

"Um…because I like music?"

"The only women who whistle are witches," he informed me.

Moving across cultural boundaries to take up home in a new place is very hard, physically, emotionally, spiritually. My prayers already were cries to God: "Help me! Strengthen me! Guide me!" Now I had to add: "Please don't let them think I'm a witch!"

For the next several months, we all spent time getting used to each other, making room for each other's habits of the heart as well as of the culture. We became part of each other's lives. Slowly, I adapted and then adopted major chunks of their culture into my life. Slowly, they adapted to and then adopted me.

After a while, it was the children who let me know the adaptation and adoption were complete, that I was no longer the outsider, that no one thought I was a witch.

One of my best friends, a seven-year-old, came to me.

"I like it when you whistle. Can you teach me?"

GOD THE MUSIC LOVER
CAMILLE HEGG

My mother was the musician in my family. She would sit at the Steinway grand piano her parents had bought for her when she was four and play "name that tune" with us kids.

She might choose to play a jingle from a commercial, a tune from her vast collection of records from the forties, a Bach invention, a Beethoven sonata, a Christmas carol, or a hymn. We kids got so good that we could sometimes name the piece in just a few notes. Sometimes we got to "name that tune" and she played whatever we named.

She taught us about strong beats, time, flats, sharps, minor and major keys. Human emotions are reflected in music and rhythm. Humans can sing, praise, dance, clap, give thanks, rejoice, lament, weep—respond to the events of life with God's intricate gift of music and rhythm.

Mother helped us understand that music is more than notes or words. All musical instruments have their special sounds and rhythms. Silence and space also are part of the music that is life.

God has placed in Creation an intricate system of music, rhythm, sounds, and rests. When I listen deeply I know there are rhythms of life that make their own kind of music. Crickets chirp and lightning bugs light with their own kinds of rhythm. Tree frogs croak in a rhythm each night. Are they communicating with each other? And cicadas, every seventeen years? How do they know? Amazing.

When my daughter was a baby I sang to her. Then I sang to her children, my grandchildren. Sometimes they ask me to sing "that song." It's totally made up, but it is rhythmical, it is theirs, and created in love.

God is a music lover with a vast repertoire.

Virtue is not the sign of a Christian. Joy is.
—MADELEINE L'ENGLE

GLASS CEILING

LAUREN R. STANLEY

When I was eight, my mother gave me the awful news: I would not grow up to be the starting catcher for the Chicago Cubs in the World Series. Not because they were cursed or awful, nor because the Mets were so amazing, but because I was a little girl, and little girls did not play for the Chicago Cubs.

This was the first time my mother told me I couldn't be whatever I wanted to be. Always, she had encouraged me: *You can grow up to do anything.* Now, she added that devastating word: *Except...*

When I was ordained, I crashed into that glass ceiling again...

It wasn't the last time someone told me no. For years, I was a newspaper editor. Working on the sports desk, I was told I couldn't possibly understand sports, even though I played, watched, and practically breathed them. I couldn't edit NASCAR, even though I was one of the few who knew the difference in carburetor lift between the Daytona and Talladega Superspeedways.

When I was ordained, I crashed into that glass ceiling again: *You can't work for a woman rector, because there can't be two women at the altar. You can't be rector of a large parish, because those jobs go to men. You can't be a missionary in much of the world, because much of the Anglican world does not ordain women.*

You can't...you can't...you can't...

I never listened to those voices, because I knew that God was calling me into these fields. I heard a clear call to "follow me," and I did, bumping and banging into those glass ceilings, sometimes smashing them.

All the voices were wrong. Except my mother's. She knew, long before I did, that being the starting catcher for the Chicago Cubs in the World Series was not my call after all.

WORKING IT OUT
SARA D. PINES

Commitment and desire go hand in hand. Waking up one morning and deciding to become a surgeon when your education and experience are in the accounting field is desire. After you investigate the courses you'll have to take, the training you'll undergo, the cost in money and time to achieve that desire, you'll discover whether you have the commitment to follow through.

The rich young ruler described in Luke's Gospel woke up that morning with the desire for something better in his life. He started the investigative process, going to Jesus and asking, "What can I do to be saved?" He discovered that he didn't have the commitment to make it happen.

Saying that what stands between us and our desires is our commitment of time and money might sound like a church's stewardship sermon. It's more personal than that.

When I whined that I had not completed my college education and was now too old to do it, a friend pointed out that I was forty-four years old and that could not change. But it was my choice to be forty-four and uneducated or forty-four and educated. I found the commitment to finish my education while working and taking care of my household. Taking classes on the weekend, using the The College Level Examination Program (CLEP), and receiving credit for one class by examination got me through in two years.

Sometimes you can only take baby steps to your goal (desire) because of family commitments or money commitments. Waiting for the other commitments to be resolved or to go away is procrastination. You can work it out. Explore the possibilities.

When the rich young ruler was confronted with an all-or-nothing situation, his choice was to walk away. We don't know what his other commitments were. Maybe he took some baby steps. Maybe he started the biblical equivalent of a soup kitchen or a homeless shelter with the money and power he refused to relinquish to Jesus. It's a possibility. What's yours?

WOMEN MAKING PEACE
MARGARET ROSE

In the summers when I was a child, all the cousins would come for a week to visit my grandmother. When the evening meal got rowdy, as it often did with so many around the table talking of politics, religion, and sports, my Aunt Roberta would grab a fly swatter and wave it over the assembled company. "We are going to have a nice, quiet meal," she declared. And our conversations immediately became civil.

I always wondered what it would be like if Aunt Roberta were at the peace talks in Jerusalem or Iran or Paris. What if women whose voices had made peace in the family for years—who brought estranged members together for a meal and who said clearly that we would be at peace for the eating—were offering those voices at the tables where women and men were sent to war?

> The women's work did not stop until there was a truce among the warring parties.

And then I met Amelia Ward from Liberia. She and others started the Mano River Peace Initiative there. Women went out into the bush to speak to child soldiers, essentially telling them "to go home to their families for dinner." The women's work did not stop until there was a truce among the warring parties.

And not long afterwards Ellen Johnson Sirleaf, who still presides over a fragile peace, was elected President of Liberia. This is not to say that women are naturally more peace-loving or more nurturing than the men who are our leaders. But the roles women have played in families and in the private realms of our culture will certainly change the conversation as they are lived out in the public realm of governments and communities.

I think of it as the Aunt Roberta voice for peace, but the truth is that it is the voice of Jesus calling us to civil discourse, to hearing and to listening, as we share bread and wine or a common meal.

MESSES TO MAKE
CAMILLE HEGG

Because I am a baker I have various kinds of flour on hand at any given time. My grandchildren watch me knead dough and ask to help. They add the ingredients to feed the two different sourdough starters I have going all the time. They smell the rosemary, basil, and mint growing. They pour cinnamon and stir in raisins. The older grandchild puts cheese onto dough that she has kneaded with a little guidance from me. She covers it with grated cheese and rolls it up, somewhat.

The little one asks to "use flour." As she moves the stool and takes her place in front of the shallow sheet cake pan I place for her on the counter, she is the conductor of a symphony about to happen in the form of flours. She adds white flour, wheat, nine-grain, and rye and enjoys the different textures and colors. The pale yellow of semolina is fascinating to her. As if finger painting, she makes drawings and spells words with her hands and fingers. She erases them all and begins again.

Her flour art and music can't be contained. As she works, a fine flour cloud rises and lands on the counter and floor. She spells her name or draws on the counter. That is a different feeling, too. She is creating. The mess is cleaned up and she helps do that, too. Our new ritual.

What if messes weren't allowed?

God took earth, air, fire, water, elements like gold and aluminum, sodium and chloride, colors and textures, plants and animals, and made Creation. Beauty, chaos theory, quantum physics, atoms and protons, gravity and intelligence all go into the art and music that is Creation.

What seems messy and disorderly can evolve into something new and hopeful.

Messes allowed!

INVIDIA
CAROL MCCREA

Invidia is the Latin word for envy, the green-eyed monster.

I admit it. I'm envious. Of prettiness. Pretty feet, well-turned ankles, slim, noncellulite thighs. All the things I don't have, I now stare at wistfully. Never knew I had envy before. I thought envy had to do with people's money, houses, cars, husbands, or clothes—external things. But my envy is more internal, and it owns me.

I was sick with envy over my godchild before I had a baby of my own. I went through a rough period of house envy during the McMansion boom when I lived in the wealthiest county in the United States. The character defect sat sizzling inside me, and I was blind to it.

Of course I blamed my mother for commenting on people's perfect noses, athletic grace, or shapely legs and "making" me feel deficient, intensely disappointing, and unloved.

Now I own it. It's my envy. Mom didn't cause it. It's my response to her comments. And it is extremely uncomfortable, as are all Ten Commandment violations. A loving God wants me to avoid envy the way a good parent would

The character defect sat sizzling inside me, and I was blind to it.

like her child to avoid harming herself. For my own comfort and well-being, I can rid myself of envy in the time-honored way, as I did with the McMansions: admit my envy to myself, God, and another human being (in this case, that would be you) and humbly ask God to remove it.

I confessed my McMansion envy to my pastor. He suggested I enjoy beautiful houses as architecture, a feast for my eyes. I followed his advice and eventually the envy left and the enjoyment remained. Perhaps I will one day do that with human bodies: enjoy their beauty and praise their architect—God.

BREADWINNING
SARAH BRYAN MILLER

When I was a little girl, some decades ago, fathers worked in offices and mothers worked keeping house, cooking meals, and raising children, and played bridge on selected afternoons.

> Women's incomes are rarely optional now; what was supposed to be a choice twenty-five years ago has become a necessity.

The mother of one girl in my Brownie troop was divorced and had a full-time job. She "had to work." No one talked about it; everyone felt immensely sorry for her.

Unlike most of my classmates, I always knew that my mother had a profession—librarian—and, unlike most of my classmates' mothers, didn't have to go back to school to finish a degree when the time came to look for a job. Eventually that time came for most of them.

When we finished high school, more of us knew the importance of getting an education and having a way to support ourselves. More of us worked when our children were young—eyebrows were even raised in some quarters when I took seasons off from singing in the opera when my daughters were born—and few of us played bridge.

Women's incomes are rarely optional now; what was supposed to be a choice twenty-five years ago has become a necessity. That's especially true for me; for the last twelve years, I've been the sole or primary earner in this household, the last two of them after divorcing. I am blessed in having work at which I'm good and which I enjoy, but with pay cuts and a poor economy, it's a financial juggling act.

I often wish that my breadwinning were a shared responsibility, that this burden were not all on my shoulders alone. But times change, circumstances change, and we must change with them. Thanks be to God for the gifts of ability, of access to jobs and other roles that challenge and fulfill us, and for the adaptability to accept change of all kinds.

FLIRTING

LAUREN R. STANLEY

My mother was French. From an early age, she taught me the fine art of flirting. "This is how we communicate," she said. With smiles. With laughter. With genuine warmth. She would flirt with anyone, and made friends everywhere she went. "It's a way of life," she'd say.

As I grew older, I flirted as well. "You make friends wherever you go," people would say. "How do you do that?"

"I flirt," I'd reply. "My mother taught me."

Years later, serving as a missionary in Sudan, the fine art of flirting kept me from being thrown into a jail I was desperate to avoid. I was being evacuated from the country, but needed an exit visa. No government official wanted to help. My visa was invalid, they told me. (Not true.) My passport had expired, they said. (Also not true.) We need to arrest you, they threatened. You are going to jail, they warned in very cold tones.

> I knew what I was doing. I was flirting my way out of jail.

Please, I would say in Arabic, with a small smile, I need your help. I have to return to the United States. There's a family emergency.

The flirting would commence…a smile here, a small gesture there, an intentional mispronunciation of key words, followed by an offer to help me learn the language better, a discussion of what I liked best about Sudan and the Sudanese people, much laughter.

My Southern Sudanese friends did not understand, but I assured them I knew what I was doing. I was flirting my way out of jail.

Eight offices, eight officials, eight instances of flirting large and small…

Forty-eight hours later, I had my exit visa, as well as eight new friends.

"This is how we communicate," I told my friends. With smiles. With laughter. With genuine warmth.

It's a way of life.

Motherhood

MARY: THE FIRST PRIEST
RUTH LAWSON KIRK

After my first natural child-birthing, the nurse who had placed my son to my breast returned again an hour later. She had heard that I was a priest, and having been raised as a Roman Catholic, she was curious about me. Never having met a woman priest, she could not imagine me, but even more because I knew and used language she didn't believe any priest would utter.

> I knew and used language she didn't believe any priest would utter.

I was not aware that I had sworn through the travail of labor until that moment. After a good laugh, all I could do was assure her that Roman Catholic priests also both knew those curses and used them from time to time. So much for holy behavior, I thought.

I pondered more. Though honest, those four-letter utterances did not defile the beauty of labor's pain. I participated in the same work as Mary, though surrounded by modern conveniences. I gave birth to a child of God, holy and blessed. My firstborn son was wrapped in clean cotton flannel; my husband was just as loyal and true as Joseph; and my son was visited by many who rejoiced at the news of his birth.

And in a quiet moment, as I held his tiny sleeping form, a sword pierced my heart as I saw that I could not protect him from the onslaughts of life's tormentors.

So I prayed, gratitude and petition blending in their own sweet song.

The Mother of our Lord became real to me in those hours. She became the first priest, offering the life of Jesus for God's people. In pain and grief, in nurture and release, Mary sanctified my labor and delivery.

My soul magnifies the Lord. Let it be with me according to your word.
—LUKE 1:46, 38

HANGING ON YOUR HEART STRINGS

HELEN L. HOOVER

"I get so tired of the kids being under my feet all the time," I told an older friend, Effie, as I washed clothes, fixed meals, tidied up the kitchen, and made the beds. My young children managed to stay close by and in my way with a million questions and pleas for my attention.

"Oh, Helen," Effie replied sorrowfully, "when the kids are young they hang on your apron strings, but when they are older, they hang on your heart strings."

> I still hurt when my children hurt, but they make their decisions now, not me.

Her comment got my attention at the time, but I didn't comprehend what she meant. Forty years later, I now understand what Effie was telling me.

I still hurt when my children hurt, but they make their decisions now, not me. When sickness strikes, I pray and wait for them to call with the good or bad news. When they are treated unjustly at work, I cannot intervene for them. I ache when the grandchildren have problems, but resolving those problems falls now on their parents' shoulders. I am still available for advice and some assistance, but the main responsibility for raising children has passed from my life.

Whether grown children live close by or thousands of miles away, the strings to a parent's heart remain tied securely. I pray for my children, enjoy them as adults, and watch their lives unfold. Yet the strings still tug and pull.

My heart stays intact, even with the tugging, because I rely on God to guide my children through the plan he has for their life.

> *For surely I know the plans I have for you, says the LORD,*
> *plans for your welfare and not for harm,*
> *to give you a future with hope.*
> —JEREMIAH 29:11

"HE KNOWS WHO HIS MOTHER IS"
ANNE O. WEATHERHOLT

These words of wisdom from another working mother have been a touchstone for me, one that I fondled and kept in the pocket of my soul. I still remember the day I went back to work, leaving my first baby with an excellent day care mother, but leaving him nevertheless. Guilt sat on my shoulders, on my plate, in my gut, and everywhere else it could sit. Would he remember that I left him in the care of someone else? Would he be okay?

> Guilt sat on my shoulders, on my plate, in my gut, and everywhere else it could sit.

Would he listen to me, wait for me, miss me? Would he grow up "her" child or mine? I wept.

After days of worry, days of swinging between guilt when I left and relief when I returned, I confided in another working mother with a school-aged child. Over lunch, which soon became soaked with my tears, she murmured, "He knows who his mother is!"

As time went on, I found her words were true. Years later, both of my sons still know who their mother is, but also benefit from the extra love of "other mothers" who still see them at church and around our small town.

Jesus knew who his mother was.

With his last breaths, "Woman, here is your son," he gave care of his mother to the beloved disciple. Looking through eyes clouded with sweat and tears, he knew the one who had given him birth, who had opened her heart to the joyful and painful thrust of love and guilt. Into the hands of God she committed him, so he might bring us all into the hands of God.

DAUGHTERS
SARAH BRYAN MILLER

I always wanted a daughter. Oh, I was fine with the idea of having a boy as well, but if I could have only one baby, I wanted a girl.

When my daughters were born, we were all ecstatic. I, too, was blessed in being wanted and valued.

Such pleasure in the birth of girls is distinctly unusual. In many cultures, and even here in the West, boys are often more desired. My mother was never allowed to forget her lapse in being born without a Y chromosome, and I have heard acquaintances complain about their own lack of sons (or grandsons) as if it were a failure of some sort. We all know what happened to Anne Boleyn.

In some parts of the world the devaluation of women goes much further. In villages in India, traveling ultrasound machines have led to the abortions of unborn girls; in China, buckets of water are often placed next to the birthing bed, for the efficient disposal of female infants. In 2005, a study estimated that more than 90 million girls were "missing" from a wide swath of Asian countries, from Afghanistan to Korea, due to selective infanticide.

My daughters and I don't always agree on the paths they should take in life, but I cannot imagine my life without them. They were a blessing to me as they grew and developed and came to maturity.

> My mother was never allowed to forget her lapse in being born without a Y chromosome.

Christians should be more enlightened on the subject of women than most; we have Christ's example of valuing and reaching out to women in a culture that treated them as chattel. "There is no longer Jew or Greek, there is no longer slave or free, there is no longer male and female; for all of you are one in Christ Jesus," says Galatians 3:28.

Amen to that.

FORCED TO GROW UP
CAROL MCCREA

What was the most difficult thing to me about raising kids? First, I was shocked that they would fight so much. As an only child for seventeen years, I didn't experience sibling rivalry or aggression. It still surprises me when people are aggressive toward me. In families with more than one child, each learns early about rivalry and aggression, and I believe it prepares them for the outside world the way puppies' play-fighting prepares them.

Furthermore, I didn't realize parenting would be so exhausting. Sleep-deprived until my kids went to college, I relish my sleep today and see it as a compensating gift for separation from them. Early on, it was even difficult to shower solo, not to mention toileting with kids howling outside the bathroom door.

Having kids is God's plan for *me,* whereby I am finally forced to grow up.

Far worse was the realization that I wasn't as patient, loving, or even as grown-up as I had believed. Having waited until my thirties to have kids, I couldn't even plead youth and inexperience. I hated when I couldn't talk to a friend, be on the phone, have time to read or think. If I was focused on something else, I hated to pull myself away when asked a question by my family. "Don't-anybody-interrupt me" was my mantra.

As I am writing this, someone may ask me something, and I will struggle to raise my eyes from the computer, put down the paper, or tear myself away from the program. This is my will run rampant.

Yet, having kids is God's plan for *me,* whereby I am finally forced to grow up.

And I suppose that is why the Lord's Prayer is my favorite, perhaps because Jesus himself prayed it and told us to do the same. There is another reason: it's about God's will rather than mine.

HERE'S GRANDMA
WESTINA MATTHEWS

"Where's Grandma?" I heard my daughter ask my nine-month-old granddaughter. Big, brown, saucer eyes turned toward me and smiled. My heart broke open in joy and wonder.

As I reached for her, I remembered a conversation with my own mother so many years ago. In one of our late-night telephone conversations, I quietly confessed to her that when I died and got to heaven, the first question that I intended to ask God was why I didn't have any children. "Why me, Lord? Why did I never have a child?"

How could God have made a woman so loving and caring, whose arms ached to hold a child of her own, and yet decide that she was not to have one?

A prayer partner once reminded me that God's will is what you would choose if you knew all the facts. Because I rarely know all the facts, I still find myself at times being willful, wanting my way on my timetable. And yes, at times my faith still wavers; in those times it becomes difficult to understand—let alone accept—God's will for me.

> "Why me, Lord? Why did I never have a child?"

Yet, fifteen years later, my nine-month-old granddaughter is reaching out her chubby arms to give me a slobbery baby kiss. Handing her over to me is my "adopted" daughter-by-another-mother who entered my life when she was a seventeen-year-old college intern at my then job. One evening over dinner, we adopted each other, becoming the family each of us yearned to have but seemed to have been denied.

"Here's Grandma," I cooed softly. "Come to Grandma."

God's will is what you would choose if you knew all the facts.

A CHILD'S STRENGTH
TARA LYLE

Children are a heritage from the LORD,
and the fruit of the womb is a gift.
—PSALM 127:3

I have wondered at times what my daughters think about my parenting skills, but I have been too afraid to ask. I've sometimes compared being a parent with being a child of God. I have found that being a parent is one of the most fulfilling roles I could have ever had, yet it has also been one of the most painful roles.

My heart was broken because I couldn't reverse the fact that I shot and killed my husband.

I am blessed to have two wonderful daughters, both in their twenties. I feel that God gave me my best fit as a mother. I couldn't imagine being incarcerated and not having them in my life.

Before I was imprisoned, I devoted my life to my family. Even though my marriage was rocky, I loved my girls to the best of my ability. I supported them in their endeavors and, like many parents, wanted them to have an easier life and more opportunities than I did. Their unconditional love inspired me beyond my measure. The pain I experienced surrounding my daughters stemmed from the poor decisions I made that forever changed the landscape of our family.

My heart was broken because I couldn't reverse the fact that I shot and killed my husband. The devastation would have a lasting effect upon my daughters' futures. My mistakes had far-reaching consequences on their lives. When so many lives are shattered, only God's unconditional love and grace can help us rebuild our lives.

My daughters have suffered needlessly, but the amazing grace of God has also sustained them in their weakest moments. Out of love for me, they have shielded me from many of the disappointments, frustrations, and wounds they have had to endure. My girls forgave me out of love, and it is that love that has breathed new life into me. The most important acts I do as an incarcerated mother are to pray for my children often, keep the lines of communication open, and never let them forget how much I love them.

I behold God's mercy and grace through the love of my precious daughters.

RECONCILIATION
ANGELA BOATRIGHT-SPENCER

Mothers and daughters have issues; my mother and I were no different. She was a light-skinned black woman with naturally straight hair—two facts of which she was proud. I have my father's dark coloring and gloriously kinky hair. My mother never seemed to see the person I was. She was "shocked" upon learning that someone wanted to marry me. See what I mean? We had issues.

> I ask her, softly, if there is anything she would like to say to God, speaking now as the daughter who also is a priest.

Mom loved to daydream. She would sit at her window for hours, one eye on the clouds, traveling back to when her mother—her best friend—was alive. My mother's mind deteriorated quickly; she was firmly in the land of dementia long before entering the valley of the shadow of death. We placed her in a nursing home. People dressed her up and did her nails—it was an existence she seemed to love. She was the staff's sweetheart; they puzzled over the daughter who rarely visited this sweet old woman.

Decades pass. I look like her, gray hair and all, just darker, and she thinks I'm her sister. She has stopped eating. The doctor wants to put in a feeding tube. I'm there to see how she is, *where* she is. I sit beside the bed. Her glance flits from one spot on the ceiling to another, as if she's watching fireflies against a summer evening sky. I've seen patients near death do that before; it has convinced me that God sends someone to us so we don't die alone. Perhaps she is seeing her mother.

I try feeding her a drink, but the liquid slides out of her mouth. She's forgotten how to swallow. I ask her, softly, if there is anything she would like to say to God, speaking now as the daughter who also is a priest. Her eyes remain fixed on the ceiling. I say the confession, begin the absolution. Her head turns and her eyes lock on mine. She isn't just looking, she's actually *seeing* me. There's a *knowing* on her face. Just as I say, "I absolve you from all your sins," her eyes flicker and go blank, as if someone had turned off a switch. And she is gone.

And so, somehow, is the barrier separating us. In that one glance, years of estrangement became irrelevant. *I remember them, but they don't matter.* Her ashes sit on a shelf in my house; a golden angel rests on top of the golden box containing them.

All shall be well, and all shall be well,
and all manner of thing shall be well.
—MOTHER JULIAN OF NORWICH

My first granddaughter isn't

Cynthia Caruso

Sofia Marie will be born in February, maybe on my birthday, and she will be my first grandchild, or rather, my first grand-goddaughter. Her mother, Valerie, is a former student who transferred to Comfort my last year of teaching in Texas, when I was depressed and so was she.

Valerie came to live with her father in our small town, but that didn't work out, and she lived with a boyfriend for a while, then called me and asked in her small voice, "Can I live with you, Mrs. Caruso?" I was very depressed and afraid to take on any responsibility, so I told her that she could live with me, but I couldn't vet her boyfriends and I didn't cook.

I needn't have worried. Val did it all. She enrolled in alternative school and finished two and one-half years of school in nine months. She qualified for Medicaid and got a job at Sonic. In six months she moved into an apartment with a friend. Two months later her mother took an accidental overdose of Vioxx. She is now in a Missouri nursing home, brain-dead. Val came over nearly every day, to drink Peet's coffee and talk. Then Luis began to take her out, and soon they were talking of marriage.

I gave her a wedding, and before she got married, she was baptized. I became her godmother, and after the wedding, Val and Luis moved in with me, until I left on my first Big Adventure. Val has had two miscarriages, but now she is six months along.

> I told her that she could live with me, but I couldn't vet her boyfriends and I didn't cook.

I sympathize with the disciples who were terrified when they saw Jesus walking toward them on the water. They had never seen such a thing before, and it took them a while to recognize their Lord. I was afraid, too, when I took Valerie in, but it didn't take me long to realize that God had entered with her.

God must be part woman

Janet F. Fuller

I was pregnant for ten years, waiting—
sweetly, bitterly, anxiously—for the child
God would give me. I tried every medical
treatment, every surgical and pharmaceutical
option, suffered miscarriages, the monthly
empty cramping signaling my failure. I was
barren, like Sarah. Thank you, God, that I did not have to wait ninety years
as she did.

I was pregnant for ten years, waiting— sweetly, bitterly, anxiously—for the child God would give me.

Hope, success, and failure are built into our physical selves as women. Hope
has a life of its own in us. Every new moon is a new set of possibilities. Every
menstrual period is a sign of failure, but offering yet again a period of hopeful
anticipation. Every bodily twinge is a possible signal of our best dreams or
dashed hopes.

In the end it was by adoption that I became a mother. My son Sam was a gift
out of a dark, lonely mountain village. I know this, even now that he is seventeen
and a wretched teenager. He came, not from my body, but from my heart. He is
not my blood, but completely mine. His origins are a mystery; my love for him
has equally mysterious origins.

God must be part woman. She waited in anxious hope for our arrival. She
adopted us into her family from sorry shelters where we waited for a saving love.
She didn't mind if we didn't look like her. She waits in hope, even now, for me to
acknowledge her gifts, her tangled love and sorrow for me. She never gives up on
me, even when she doesn't like me.

Does she also feel that I am a gift to her life? That even in wretchedness I am
completely hers in love?

Does she want me to crawl into her lap and rest a while in silent sharing?

I'm ready.

THE CHILDREN OF OUR HEARTS

NOËL JULNES-DEHNER

When I was in high school, I decided I would adopt a child. During college at the height of the Vietnam War, I felt drawn toward international adoption.

A year into our marriage I was pregnant—until I miscarried on my birthday.

Before marrying, my husband and I discussed international adoption, and he was all for it. Because we were in our thirties, we planned to have a biological child first. A year into our marriage I was pregnant—until I miscarried on my birthday. For many years I didn't recognize my depression on my birthdays as my body and soul grieving. I began side-effect laden fertility drugs, and as I sat in the doctor's waiting room one morning, I felt a conviction that I would have twins.

Enrolled in a dream analysis class, I deciphered that I would not have biological children. The professor disagreed with my interpretation, but it turned out to be accurate. The most powerful dream I had was in May, when I asked to dream about my children. I dreamt that I was with a woman in South America and then went to Germany.

Unknown to us, in June our twins were born in Paraguay, of Hispanic and German heritage. We didn't file our adoption paperwork until November.

On Christmas Eve, our rector preached about the joy of being at the birth of each of his five children, the most painful sermon I have ever endured. We cried when we arrived home. Where was God for people like us?

The day after Epiphany the call came: would we be interested in twins? While we were crying on Christmas Eve, our malnourished daughters were arriving at the Paraguayan adoption lawyer's house, in search of a family.

Looking back we see the subtle signs announcing their arrival. Twenty-five years ago the children of our hearts came home. Our love and gratitude have expanded ever since.

ON FERTILITY AND TURNING FORTY
ERIN MARTINEAU

Spending the last year learning to farm, I'm struck by the insisting insistence of life, the yearning to reproduce, to live on, to flower forth. The cool-weather crops sensed the rising heat of summer, and "bolted" toward new life, sending out seedpods faster than we could trim them back. The tomatoes ripened faster than we could catch them, their seeds splashing into the soil. I know we'll see their offspring next summer.

I am turning forty, and I know that my body won't ever bear children.

Our futile attempts to manage, pace, control the fertility of the garden are almost comical, and I find myself just shaking my head as I carry out from the garden armloads of plants gone to seed. Earth pushes forth her marvelous gifts, and we are simply overwhelmed, racing to keep up, to create a little order in the blooming chaos of generativity.

I am turning forty, and I know that my body won't ever bear children. Even though this is a choice I have made, I can feel the pulsing of life in my body—my womb has some mysterious connection to the fertility of these fields. And I ache for all the thwarted seedpods, now tossed in a compost heap, though I know that they will become life in a new form, will birth themselves into being, rich soil. I am grateful I can sense that my life force will bear fruit, even if not a child.

My body knows that the clock is winding down. It is an exquisite longing, this drive to reproduce. I honor it, this drumbeat, this deepest of urges, as the pulse of life itself within me, linking me to the life force that hums through all Creation.

ADVENT MORNING
ANNE KITCH

*For you yourselves know very well that
the day of the Lord will come like a thief in the night.*
—1 THESSALONIANS 5:2

The girls have left for school and the sudden stillness fills the house. Although this has been going on for months, my husband and I find each other slightly bewildered at the calm. This year our daughters are walking to school by themselves. No more rushing everyone out the door all at the same time. It is amazing how much difference five minutes to myself can make. Even if I leave for work immediately before or after the girls leave, our morning routine is so much easier. They get themselves organized and out the door. I am only responsible for myself.

The first day of school we walked together. And they totally ditched me at Broad Street. The light at the crosswalk was about to change as we approached, and with not-quite-so-furtively-exchanged glances, they ran for it. They waved to me from across the street and continued on their way, as I was forced to stand and wait for the light to change again. I smiled. Later I cried.

I anticipate with delight the compassion and creativity they will add to the world.

They are growing up. This is not news to me. "You spend the first six years of a child's life trying to keep hold of her," said my mother, "and the next six years learning to let go." But I find myself unprepared. Their moving into such independence has always seemed so far off. It's as if a thief came in the night and snuck their childhood out the door while I was sleeping.

It is the fear of loss rather than the change itself that makes transitions difficult. I want them to grow into the wonderfully mature women that God has created them to be. I anticipate with delight the compassion and creativity they will add to the world. And I do live in expectation of the coming of Christ the King. But I am still afraid of losing them.

Natural highlights

Lynn Fairfield

I'd never had it done but watched and winced
As Debbie jabbed, then pulled and combed with care
Some slender strands of Kate's wet, curly hair
Through foil—a metal fitted shower cap.
Her skillful hands tight-gloved against the burn,
She painted each now-separate strand with bleach
And left, to let it eat its lightening way
Into the born-brown, sturdy pigment strip.
Once dried and rinsed and cut and styled,
The hair, in ordinary light, looked spun
Or shot with threads of gold and sun, alive.
And Kate was pleased; she looked light-crowned she said.
I wished my thankfulness to God would show
As subtly bright as Kate's new highlights glow.

BETWEEN US
JUDITH HOLLOWAY BAUM

Hurt inflicted usually springs from hurt endured.
With this in mind, I choose to ignore your words
    written boldly, blackly on your sheer flowered paper.
Apologies if I offended you with my advice.
It is by farther climbing that I can see the horizon
    more clearly than you.
You must forgive a mother's gentle boosting
And I'll forgive a daughter's yearning to pause along
    the way.

O Holy Wisdom, soaring Power,
encompass us with wings unfurled,
and carry us, encircling all,
above, below, and through the world.
—HILDEGARD OF BINGEN

CHAPTER

At the Altar

STAINS ON MY ALB • TALITHA CUM: LITTLE GIRL, GET UP

ON WANTING YOU TO TAKE MY FUNERAL

LORD, HEAR OUR PRAYER • THE CROSS OF CHRIST

RADIANT LIGHT • DISHING UP HOLY FOOD AND DRINK

STAINS ON MY ALB
ANNE O. WEATHERHOLT

Spread like empty crucifix, my alb rests

not on the flat space of sacristy preparation

but on white porcelain of a washday tub.

Examine each part, observe stories expressed.

Mist gently, ablution for absolution.

Around the collar, uneven pattern of stain,

intense legacy of funereal paradox: grief and hope.

At each shoulder, beige joy pressed by faces,

darker red of lips—a head buried in sorrow.

Around each cuff, rubbings: wrists lifted high, tucked low,

repetitious offering.

At the front, small splash, left as trace of blood on a bandage.

Under each arm, warm scents of labor,

midwifery of liturgy and word; honest toil of birthing souls.

Along the sides, erasure from smaller hands of children,

smudge of crayon tucked in tiny hands at sacramental rail.

At the hem, dark trail, catch of heels folded under,

obeisance to the mystery of reserved holiness.

The stains on my alb mix with the water that dilutes and purifies

all outward signs of inward grace.

The palette fresh for the next portrait:

giving, sharing,

holding, letting go,

lifting up, bowing low,

dance of vocation caught in the mundane.

TALITHA CUM: LITTLE GIRL, GET UP

RUTH LAWSON KIRK

I love the story of her rising. On the verge of womanhood, a girl child dies.

She is beloved by her father enough for him to risk his status as a leader of the synagogue to make a public petition of the wonder-working rabbi who speaks so much of God. She is mourned by the people who wail at the announcement of her death. Taking only the closest disciples and her parents, Jesus is surrounded by love and faith. He takes her by the hand and calls to her. From death to life, from grief to joy, from childhood to womanhood, our unnamed girl rises, holding the hand of Jesus.

> I could become what I imagined I would be...

Talitha cum, I heard. I was twelve and sweltering in the oppressive summer's heat when the Philadelphia eleven[*] were ordained. On the verge of womanhood, I heard Jesus speak to me through *The New York Times,* in the image of my Episcopal sisters rising into priesthood. It was my mother who took me by the hand and told me to get up. I could become what I imagined I would be, rising from childhood to womanhood, ordained as the priest and pastor she never could be.

I hear it still. When I'm frightened and unsure, feeling smaller than a woman, I hear the voice telling me, *Talitha cum.* Sometimes the voice sounds like my mother's, whose speech has been swallowed up by Alzheimer's these past three years. All my life she had the power to speak the healing, rising, empowering words of Jesus to me. She speaks them still. Sometimes the voice is deeper and sweeter still, calling me from death to life, from fear to trust, from weakness to strength. "Little girl, get up!"

And I do. I will. With God's help.

---

[*] The "Philadelphia eleven" were eleven female deacons who were irregularly ordained to the priesthood on July 29, 1974. This event forced the question of women's ordination in the Episcopal Church and its eventual approval by the General Convention of the Episcopal Church in September 1976.

ON WANTING YOU TO TAKE MY FUNERAL
LYNN FAIRFIELD

Accompany me, my feet first, and touch the bier
Where I repose transposed to celestial time.

Stay, please. Spread the warm, silken pall.
Remind the mourners of the body's goodness.
Wear the white and gold, your Albion threads
Soon to be subsumed in Light of Light.

Keep the feast with the family for me.
Break the bread; face them faith forward.
Describe a cross, nose to heart, with incense,
If you must, must to musk, masking all decay.

Speak loudly, your Cranmer cadences not for
Me but for the living, yearning for the Word.
Crumble clods of mudpie earth and throw them
Down, flung to reverberate through ash or bone.

Read out the sure and certain hope, hope
To Whom, head first, you'll follow me someday.

Christ has no body now but yours,
No hands, no feet on earth but yours.
Yours are the eyes through which he looks
compassion on this world.
Christ has no body now on earth but yours.
—TERESA OF AVILA

LORD, HEAR OUR PRAYER
WANDA RUTH COPELAND

Week by week we pray the Prayers of the People in our worship. We pray for the bishop, for those in congregations around the world, the homeless, and those celebrating special occasions.

I love the consolidated prayers of the congregation. Echoing through time, they bind all God's people—from north to south and east to west—with the saints. They are soothing, powerful, righteous. And it feels good to say, "Lord, hear our prayer."

> We were so accustomed to giving, so very unprepared to receive.

I remember when it became my turn, when we prayed for my husband, Tom. It was unsettling to hear his name, to know that the entire congregation was praying for us. I was used to praying for others. Serving others was part of what we had always been about. I had no idea how it felt from the other side.

That power, that solidarity, is awe-inspiring. I remember wondering if the congregation knew what it was doing, if the people comprehended the force they were unleashing with their love. Their gesture seemed innocent enough, but the act of that good gift made both Tom and me weak in the knees. We were so accustomed to giving, so very unprepared to receive.

It's not just about a power shift. It's about growing into a new realization of the corporate affection and concern that can be mustered in such a simple act.

Prayers are felt. They matter. Prayer moves one into a whole new realm of common-unity. It was good. It remains good. Thank you.

THE CROSS OF CHRIST

BITSY AYRES RUBSAMEN

Even though I was raised in the Episcopal Church, I was encountered by our living Lord Jesus Christ on Sunday morning, October 21, 1971. It happened at our church altar rail at the conclusion of a Faith Alive weekend where lay people had come to talk about their personal relationships with Jesus. I wanted what I saw in their eyes and heard from their lips, and so I just asked Jesus to make himself real to me. Instantly he did. For the rest of the day, I was engulfed in tears and couldn't stop crying. With this conversion experience, my loving husband of fifty-three years, who had always been active in the Episcopal Church, said that, at that moment, I left him "standing in the dust."

> For in all of my "doing," I have neglected to keep my eyes focused on the cross of Christ.

Since that time, I have sought to do the things that I felt Christ called me to do, which he showed me in a vision, handing me a lunch pail on a busy intersection of highway and saying, "Feed my sheep." Shortly after, I helped to establish a diocesan hunger program and worked at that for fifteen years. I then became a chaplain on staff of a hospice for the next eight years while learning to become a spiritual director. I have continued to direct a faithful group of women these past fourteen years. And for the past six years, I have worked with a successful healing prayer ministry.

Like many women, I have "volunteered" my life away, but believe I am being who our Lord created me to be. Yet there is always the prick of the sin of pride that accompanies my daily "practice" of self-centeredness! For in all of my "doing," I have neglected to keep my eyes focused on the cross of Christ.

I'm reminded of Paul's words: "May I never boast of anything except the cross of our Lord Jesus Christ" (Galatians 6:14). I now seek to focus on the Man who chose to die on that cross for my sake and redemption.

RADIANT LIGHT
CYNTHIA CARUSO

It took my breath away, the slides of all those women, radiant on the screen of the ballroom at the convention center in Columbus, Ohio, in 2006. It was the General Convention of the Episcopal Church, and I was a delegate to Triennial. It was also the twenty-fifth anniversary of the official ordination of women, and these slides were of some of those first female ordinands.

Thank goodness the Episcopal Church moved forward decades ago.

I did not think of myself as a feminist, so I was not paying strict attention to the slide show at first. Then I looked, and I could not look away. Such joy. Such light. Women in collars, smiling. A young—all of them seemed young—blond woman was kneeling, surrounded by other women. Her eyes were closed.

I began to breathe deeply, and my nose began to prick, a sign of coming tears. How can I tell you about that light? There was so much light.

As more pictures appeared, the light continued. It was in every scene. How could I have missed it at the beginning? When the photos stopped and activity resumed, I stayed in my seat.

What if that light had never been released?

Thank goodness the Episcopal Church moved forward decades ago, taking the veil off those women and others who have followed, letting their light into the world. May the Church continue to remove the veils from all God's people, until all their light is released into the world.

DISHING UP HOLY FOOD AND DRINK
SALLY M. BROWER

Sometimes when I am feeding my flock by hand,
> whether pressing bread into tiny palms or trembling fingers,

I am overtaken by a love that
> bursts the boundaries of my carefully confined heart.

As I hold the cup to soul-parched lips thirsting for life,
> I am immersed by a compassion
> that absorbs me completely.

I stand at the table as women do,
> presiding over cups and plates and food,
> dishing up the holy food and drink of new and unending life,
> and my heart is pierced by the holy mystery,
> dazzled by the divine work I am privileged to do.

As I spread my arms, the wings of my chasuble
> gather in God's blessed brood,
> warming my own soul like a mother
> when her family is gathered in.

In this place they call me Mother,
> and so I am;
> named and claimed by the God
> whose call is love incarnate.

CHAPTER 5

Illness, Pain, and Healing

I NEED TO DANCE MORE, ALLELUIA!

WESTINA MATTHEWS

Tonight I danced to Luther, Aretha, Isaac, and Maxwell. I was on the dance floor, joining others in the Electric Slide. Alone, and yet with others. Borrowing husbands and grabbing girlfriends. Dancing, dancing, dancing.

The joy of being over fifty is that I dance now from the inside out. No longer moving from the outside in…no longer to every beat…but rather, dancing to the beat I have within. Every other beat. Every three beats. Moving slowly, but moving.

Keeping time to the beat within as the blood pumps throughout my body—over widening hips, through varicose veins, up sagging breasts, to graying hair, through dimming eyesight, and yes, around that mysterious mass in my breast.

Not thinking about tomorrow. Not even remembering yesterday. Not caring about today.

Just dancing…dancing…dancing. Popping fingers softly, swaying hips slightly, feet moving to the beat of the rhythm of my joy.

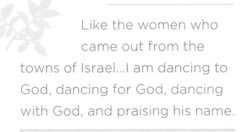

Like the women who came out from the towns of Israel…I am dancing to God, dancing for God, dancing with God, and praising his name.

Like the women who came out from the towns of Israel to meet King Saul, I am dancing to God, dancing for God, dancing with God, and praising his name. Alleluia!

Out on the dance floor, moving to the beat, eyes closed, head back, moving slowly, feeling the wonderful energy of me being *me* in the moment. Smiling, laughing, enjoying being *me.*

In this moment…I am happy. In this moment…I am free.

Pressure of job, concerns about family, house yet to be cleaned, sonogram in the wings…who cares?

All I want to do right now is dance. Feel the music pulsating within me. Dancing from the inside out. Twirling around, standing on my ground. Laughing with glee.

I need to dance more. Alleluia!

LOST COIN
MARGARET ROSE

2004. It was a year of loss: my sister dead from a brain aneurysm; eight months later my brother dead from a heart attack. Both were healthy and in their mid-fifties. Then my husband of twenty years left. It was what one might call a Job year.

In the months while I was still reeling, I received a gift from a close friend, a silver medallion necklace. The enclosed card said: "a symbol of friendship, loving and embracing you in a never-ending circle of love even as you grieve."

I treasured this gift in the knowledge that when we are suffering or in pain, there are friends and God who are our companions.

A couple of months ago, I discovered the medallion was missing. As the scripture suggests in the parable of the lost coin (Luke 15:8-10), I turned on all the lights, looked under the bed, searched pockets and drawers, felt in the crevices, and retraced my steps of the last days. It was nowhere to be found.

I must accept this loss, I said to myself. *It is only a thing after all. Let go.* I dug deeper into my heart. This must be God's way of saying, "Healing has happened. You don't need a medallion to assure you that you are loved."

A week later, however, as I pulled out a swim bag I hadn't used in a while, I felt what seemed to be a stone in the corner pocket.

And there it was.

I clasped the medallion around my neck, with renewed gratitude for the gift, for my friend, and for the healing of body, mind, and spirit blessing me over the last years. The medallion, I realized, is like the woman's lost coin, now found. I knew myself to be like that coin, found from that wounded lost place of years ago.

Thank you, God.

LOVE
ANONYMOUS

When I was a little girl growing up in New Orleans, I took classes in drama. One time when I was about seven, I had to memorize a story about an old cobbler from Marseilles. He was visited by a stranger who asked him to make a special pair of shoes for a little child who had none. Choosing his very best leather, soft and supple, the cobbler put aside his other work and labored for days on the shoes. The stranger returned and the old cobbler gave him the shoes he had so lovingly made. The stranger took them and thanked him with these words from the Gospel of Matthew:

> *For I was an hungred, and ye gave me meat:*
> *I was thirsty, and ye gave me drink:*
> *I was a stranger, and ye took me in:*
> *Naked, and ye clothed me:*
> *I was sick, and ye visited me:*
> *I was in prison, and ye came unto me.*
> *Verily I say unto you, Inasmuch as ye have done it unto one of the*
>   *least of these my brethren, ye have done it unto me.*

—Matthew 25:35-36, 40 (King James Version)

This story touched me deeply; I treasured it in my heart. Despite appearances, I grew up an abused child. I struggled, fearful and lonely. But God put special people in my life to help me through. My grandmother was one. She loved me. She was kind and gentle and had the most beautiful voice I had ever heard. My aunt was another. She occasionally tried to stand up for me even when she was cursed and maligned for doing so. There were others along the way, with occasional kind words and hugs and encouragement.

Today, after many years of healing, I marvel that we never know whose lives we may touch, sometimes bringing the love of Jesus to those who may desperately need it.

LIVING WITH ILLNESS
LINDA WALLENFANG

My husband doesn't have anything that will kill him, just peck him to death.

This is how I describe my husband to my friends when they ask me how he is feeling. I don't have words to describe how helpless I feel watching my husband of twenty-five years suffer every day with no relief in sight. What he has is not as important as how we have learned to cope with the challenges of living with chronic illness.

God is our strength and our rock. God's children (our friends) have been our soft place to land. We turn to each other with a deepening sense of commitment to God and to each other. We know that this road is not going to get any easier and my husband is going to get sicker. Our future lies not in focusing on the pain and sadness, but in focusing on the joy.

Every day we must find joy in something…anything. Proverbs 15:30 tells us: "A cheerful look brings joy to the heart, and good news gives health to the bones."

Joy is in God's Creation, in the squirrels taunting our dogs to run and get them. Joy is in our grandchildren's faces. Joy is in getting out of bed. Joy is making a meal to share together. Joy is a day with less pain. We have discovered that when we have joy in our hearts, we have hope. Hope reminds us that God is always with us, even when things seem so dark and impossible.

Lord, I ask you to fill me with all joy and peace in believing, that I may abound in hope by the power of the Holy Spirit (see Romans 15:13).

Lord Jesus, you want your joy to be fulfilled in me. Show me how you can make it happen! Lead me into it (see John 17:13).

WAITING ROOM LOVE
NOËL JULNES-DEHNER

PSA: every man's
worry—biopsy, silence
in the waiting room.

A friend's funeral is Saturday
and I scan the obituary
for his age, uncomfortably close.

On the drive here,
husband in the passenger seat,
during a time of day rarely shared:
foreign territory and language,
and I searched for topics

such as our daughter's birthday party,
weekend plans for the garden,
all verbs conjugated
in the future tense.

Twenty-five years ago
I exchanged vows
with the only man
I wanted to wait for
in grey-carpeted rooms.

You, Joseph.
Let's go home.

PRAYERS FROM THE SEASON OF BREAST CANCER
LINDSAY HARDIN FREEMAN

Awake at 4 a.m., as hot as I'd ever been—sweating, scared, dry, tossing, turning, parched in body and agonized in spirit. Four months of chemo, two more to go. Then I am in a boat. *Your boat, a fishing boat on a dark lake. Feels like the Sea of Galilee. Cool and moist nighttime air envelops me. Gone is the turmoil; your presence fills me. You are in the stern. With you, I am safe.*

Stay with me, Lord, for I am so tired. The fatigue weighs me down like a thousand rocks. One by one—or all at once—fling those rocks away that I may be made refreshed and whole again. There is much I want to do, Lord, much I need to do, much I hope you want me to do. Restore my energy and my faith; heal me in body, mind, and spirit.

God, as there is no linear time for you, I ask you to hear not just this prayer but all prayers that have been said for me since I was born. Help me to trust that those prayers still reverberate through heaven and earth, always as true as the day they were said. Those who love me here and those who stand before you now are praying for me. Incline your ear to them now. *Hear them; heal me.*

Lord, when you lived on this earth, there was a woman who had been sick for twelve years. She had spent all her money on doctors, but illness and isolation had almost won. She gathered up her strength and pushed through the crowd just to touch the hem of your robe. She knew she would be healed, and she was. Help me to have that perseverance, to keep searching. To keep going until I touch you and you heal me fully and completely, in body, mind, and spirit.

Prayer stronger than pain
Nancy R. Duvall

My husband produces kidney stones like a real pro. He has been able to pass them fairly easily for the past few years, since a doctor told him to forget about tea and drink lemonade. For years he suffered horrendous pain as the sandspur-like stones grew too large or hooked onto his passageways.

He had a bad experience with one stone too large to pass, and after all else failed, he underwent surgery to remove the stone. This was at a time when surgery meant cutting him from side to back—and major pain.

I spent the night in his room. When the medicine wore off, I realized that it would be an hour and a half before he could have more pain killers. I began to pray as I held his hand and softly rubbed his arm, just the same way, up and down, trying to reassure him.

As I prayed I remembered people he had helped during his ministry. I thanked God for each of them and thanked God that God had given Charles skills to help each one. I reminded God how much love Charles had brought to lonely, sick, and discouraged people. I called on the Holy Spirit to be with us and to help us.

Time after time during the night, the same thing happened. Charles would awake in pain, I would pray and touch him lightly, he would be able to relax and bear the pain until time for more medication. Maybe my touch helped. For sure God heard my prayers of thanksgiving for every good thing Charles had done and how much he loved the Lord.

Never again have I doubted the power of prayer.

THE *REAL* WORLD
JUDITH HOLLOWAY BAUM

Yea, though I walk through the valley of the shadow of death,
I will fear no evil: for thou art with me...
—PSALM 23:4
(KING JAMES VERSION)

The psychiatrist looked at me calmly and said, "It is quite possible to be anxious and not know it. Remember, your brain doesn't work right."

I stared at him, feeling my insides disappearing and my head swirling. Five years earlier, I had been diagnosed manic-depressive. I continued living hard and fast both professionally and socially. The "spells" came intermittently. They varied in degree and time for recovery. So great could be the fear and paranoia that I could never tell anyone what I experienced during those times. The psychotic breakdown is the mind's hell.

> The psychotic breakdown is the mind's hell.

By the time I got home, anger had replaced shock. Never had bipolar been explained to me as "the brain not working right." Always I was under the shadow of "it" happening again. Always it did. I turned my anger on God. I screamed and threw pillows and stomped the floors. I sobbed in humiliation. God listened.

Had I ever accepted that I had a mental illness? No. I tried to outrun it, outdistance it. Accept the condition, I heard. But I felt so tired, so weak, so alone.

I'll do this if you'll help me, Lord, I cried. *I can't do it by myself.*

I surrendered to God. I began to experience the *real* world of abundant living.

FAITH AND HEALING
ANONYMOUS

As a victim of childhood sexual abuse, I was good at hiding my feelings, covering up, pretending everything was okay. I lived with the pain and shame and for years I was terrified someone would find out. These things weren't talked about openly when I was a little girl; the truth of so many victims was not acknowledged. In time, the collective voices of those who were hurt were heard. Awareness of the travesty and the extent of this hidden crime against children gradually became known. Still, I never told anyone, even well into adulthood with a family of my own. The horrible secret festered inside of me.

> I never told anyone... The horrible secret festered inside of me.

I was sitting in church one Sunday morning, depressed and struggling with the pain of old wounds. Our pastor's wife was speaking that day and I couldn't believe what I was hearing! She was talking about her own experiences as a childhood sexual abuse survivor and about the healing in her life. At that moment I felt God was speaking to me, urging me to let him into the dark places, urging me to trust him. I felt I was on the edge of an abyss, about to plunge into unfathomable depths. My heart was pounding.

If I took this plunge, people would find out about the dark secret I had been hiding for so long. How could I let that happen? I thought of Abraham and how God asked him to trust, even in the face of unimaginable circumstances. I knew that the way to healing was to allow the light to shine into the dark corners of my wounded psyche. Somehow, with the Holy Spirit by my side at that moment, in my heart, I said, *Yes.* And the healing began.

> *Now faith is the assurance of things hoped for, the conviction of things not seen....By faith Abraham obeyed when he was called to set out for a place that he was to receive as an inheritance; and he set out, not knowing where he was going.*
> —HEBREWS 11:1, 8

GOD DOES NOT DESIRE MY PAIN
JANET F. FULLER

I am finally, in my early fifties, learning to stand up for myself.

Many who know me are surprised, because they have seen me as strong, perhaps even intimidating in my personal power. I was more confident in professional realms, where I could become who I most wanted to be, where I could flourish.

For twenty years I was trapped in an abusive marriage. Nobody knew that underneath the projected picture of a competent marriage, I, and later also my children, were being belittled, cursed, emotionally jerked from hostile rage to suicidal threats. The only scars were on our hearts. In growing fear and isolation, my self was whittled daily away. *I must be weak to be so paralyzed and hurt. There must be something wrong with me that my marriage is such a battlefield. I must be a failure because I can make no changes that help, although believe me, I am trying!*

I believed I was the peacemaker. I sacrificed for everyone else's welfare. I knew the fault was mine—for a rocky marriage, worried children, broken relationships, broken promises, even though I understand now that it takes two to make, keep, or break promises.

Seven years after leaving, I am beginning only now to understand the power he had. One word, a tone of voice, a look, a particular kind of silence, one broken dish, could undo me.

For twenty years I was trapped in an abusive marriage.

I am now believing that it is not my fault, that this was not God's will, that God was angry and hurt too, and glad for our escape. Every day I remind myself that I am strong. That I don't deserve to be abused. That hurt is not part of love. That God does not desire my pain. That I can stand up for myself.

Someday I will be sure of it.

BLAME
ELIZABETH BUENING

> *The LORD made his people exceedingly fruitful;*
> *he made them stronger than their enemies.*
> —PSALM 105:24

There are a lot of things we blame ourselves for that wouldn't even occur to most men: other people's feelings, uncomfortable situations, and, especially, being the victim of a crime.

When I'm heading into the emergency room to be with a survivor of sexual assault or domestic violence, I'm there as a volunteer to help her through the initial aftermath of the assault. And even though I've gone through hours of training filled with definitions and statistics, my biggest job in the emergency room is to listen and to tell the survivor that what happened to her isn't her fault. It's something we say over and over, because blaming yourself for being violated is one of the most common, shared reactions. You try to rationalize what happened—*I shouldn't have gone out with him; I should've left the party but I didn't want to make a scene.* You may even blame God—*How could you let this happen to me?* And then you ask the hardest question, "How could he/she do this to me?"

> We usually know the people who hurt us.

We usually know the people who hurt us. They know our weaknesses, abuse our trust, and violate our bodies. And in the face of that horrific truth we grasp at any rationalization that could mean it didn't happen, even if it means blaming ourselves. In church, we're taught that people are basically good and everyone deserves a second chance. But when someone is hurting you, you don't owe that person anything—not your trust, not your friendship, and certainly not a second chance.

Sexual assault and domestic violence are huge, terrifying concepts, and many people are certain they would never be in "that situation." But statistics don't lie as well as we do to ourselves. At least one in three women in the world has been beaten, raped, or otherwise abused in her lifetime, and the abuser is usually someone she knows. One in three.

Abuse isn't about love or sex; it's about power. But women are a power to be reckoned with stronger than any violence the abusers can perpetrate. With faith and perseverance we've broken down social and economic barriers, become heads of state and activists. With love and hope we raise families, run businesses and households. So with truth and our faith supporting us, let's stand up and be advocates for ourselves, and our bodies, by putting the blame where it belongs—on those who have abused us.

The woman at the well
Cathy H. George

She goes to the well at noon knowing that the women who draw water in the morning have carried their jugs home. Women will come again late in the day for water to prepare supper and wash their children. The Samaritan woman is alone at the well in the noonday heat, avoiding the humiliation of being ignored. Lost in her thoughts, she attaches her jug to the pulley and lowers it into the well. A Jewish man comes near, sits on the stone edge of the well, and asks her for water.

Sit on the stone ledge next to Jesus at the well.

Men don't come to wells. Men don't speak to women. Jews avoid Samaritans, and no one speaks to a woman like her. She hands him a cup of water from the jug she draws up from the well. And he speaks of water she will not have to walk the hot, dusty road twice a day to draw. What does he mean?

No one knows her story. Word is out, there have been five husbands, and she fetches water today for a man who will not marry her. No one knows the love she shared with her first husband, how strong and true it was, and how great her sorrow when he died so young. No one knows she had no choice but to move to his brother's bed. No one knows she would have died at the brutal hands of her third husband and so escaped to her sisters.

No one knows that laced through five men was loss and hurt, joy and dignity. But this Jewish man did; he knew it all, and he offered no ridicule. He spoke with her as if he had been there when she miscarried over and over. As if he knew there was love with the husband who called her name in the dark. *He knew everything about me.*

Talking with him in the noonday heat was like being washed in a river of living water. He spoke of himself as the Source of water that never ran dry, a fountain of fresh water in the desert welling up to eternal life.

Where can I get this living water? Where can I be understood and accepted and accompanied from the inside out?

Sit on the stone ledge next to Jesus at the well. Let yourself feel his delight in who you are, his company with you through it all, his desire for you to pour out your story in the safety of his love. Leave his presence refreshed by the water of life you carry within you. You are a tributary of living water, flowing from the great well of life.

Go find Jesus when you are at the end of your patience and strength, when you feel alone and helpless; he is waiting for you in the chapel. Tell him, "You know well what is happening, my good Jesus; I have nothing but You, who know everything. Come to my assistance." And then go, and do not worry about how you will make it through. It is enough that you have told God about it; He has a good memory.
—JEANNE JUGAN, BORN 1792

LOVE THYSELF

KAY COLLIER MCLAUGHLIN

If ever there was a passage from scripture that I *knew* I understood, this was it: "Love thy neighbor as thyself." Interpreted for me by a succession of Sunday School teachers, edicts of Southern culture, and generations of the good women of my family, it was a sure prescription for "happily ever after"—my anticipated life script.

> ...divorce ripped through my life like surgery with an old tin can lid and no anesthesia.

Along the way, some unexpected things happened, including divorce.

The late sixties found my husband and me in a church-sponsored Couples' Communications Group. Seated on pillows in a circle on the floor, I soaked up both concepts and experiences of unconditional love. Boundaries. Self-differentiation. Claiming the gifts God gave you. If my husband wasn't as enthralled as I was, he surely would grow to appreciate it all later.

Two decades later, he still hadn't, but I would need it all as divorce ripped through my life like surgery with an old tin can lid and no anesthesia.

And then God sent messages and messengers to reinforce those sixties lessons:

- The mentor who made herself available to me with the clearest boundaries I've ever known, freeing me to turn to her as I needed.

- The therapist who thundered, "Someone's been messing with your life and it is going to *stop*!"

- The outrageous shock of single adulthood after the assumed protection of marriage—demanding that I learn to say a firm *no* and take care of myself.

- The words of author Alfred Starrett: "The longer I am on the journey, the more I hear voices that speak in tongues I understand, the more I know that God-shaped void within me filled."

Then God said: "It's the syntax!"

Before I can love my neighbor I have to:

- Learn how to say *no* even when it wouldn't be considered proper or popular.

- Choose real people to be a part of my life—people who are willing to dive below life's surface with me, sharing both the adventure and the inevitable pain.

- "Love thyself"—so that I can love my neighbor.

The new commandment lives.

....

It is useless to utter fervent petitions for that kingdom
to be established and that Will be done,
unless we are willing to do something about it ourselves....
We are the agents of the Creative Spirit, in this world.
Real advance in the spiritual life, then,
means accepting this vocation with all it involves.
—Evelyn Underhill

EARTHDAY PRAYERS AND EXORCISMS
ROSEMARY RADFORD RUETHER

Great Mother Wisdom, you are the sustaining source of life and renewal of life. We forgot you. We lost touch with you, as we fled into our own minds and climbed our own hierarchies, seeking to make God in the image of our fantasies of domination over the earth, over conquered land, animals, and people. Now our folly is turning to ashes in our mouth. Our power, which we trusted to make us immortal, disconnected from body, from earth, returns to us as toxic waste and acid rain. We seek your healing touch, your nourishing presence. O Mother Wisdom, it is you on whose bosom all things lie; from your womb all things well up as from an infinite font of life. Into you all things return, falling into their many parts, to rise again from your fertile matrix as new growth, new plants, new animals.

You are the ongoing life that sustains this wondrous cycle of birth and death and rebirth again. Can we learn again to live in harmony with your ways, imitating forests and meadows that make no poisons? Our proud cities, alienated from your truth, threaten to collapse like a house of cards; nay, not so easily. How many innocent lives of birds, butterflies, furry beasts, creeping things, flying things, and swimming things will be taken down with us in our demise? Let us quiet our madness and listen to your still voice, feel your warmth pushing up between the cracks of our concrete pavements. Claim us, your erring offspring, as your own, before it is too late.

EXORCISM OF THE DEADLY SPIRITS OF POLLUTION
FROM EARTH, AIR, WATER, AND SOCIETY

EXORCISM OF EARTH

CANTOR (Chanted in plain chant, holding up a bowl of earth):

Depart, deadly spirits of pollution from our earth. We recognize you for what you are, an evergrowing threat to all life forms, to all created things. You appear on our landscapes in many forms: paper, glass, metals, and plastics. Beer cans, car hulks, nonreturnables, slag, ash, and garbage testify to our wasteful society. Even beyond our vision you lurk and poison our bodies and our world in the form of pesticides and acid rained into our soil.

Now, in repentant hope to return our earth to its healthful state, we call upon you to make way for fair earth; to remove from us all traces of your noxious presence.

Hear our cry and depart, deadly spirits of pollution!

All shout: Out, demons, out! *(drum roll, ringing bells)*

EXORCISM OF AIR

CANTOR *(Chanted in plain chant, waving a feather):*

Depart, deadly spirits of pollution from our air and skies. We recognize you for what you are, an evergrowing threat to all life forms, to all created things. You pour from paper mills and burning waste dumps, from chimneys of homes and factories, and from the exhaust pipes of automobiles and trucks. You fill our air with lethal gases, with carbon dioxide and nitrogen and sulfur oxides. Humans choke and forests die in the assault on the air we breathe.

Now in repentant hope to restore our air to its healthful state, we call upon you to make way for pure air, the life breath of all living things.

Hear our cry and depart, deadly spirits of pollution!

All shout: Out, demons, out! *(drum roll, ringing bells)*

EXORCISM OF WATER

CANTOR *(Chanted in plain chant, holding up a bowl of water):*

Depart, deadly spirits of pollution from our waters that flow upon the earth and under the earth. We recognize you for what you are, an evergrowing threat to all life forms, to all created things. You pour your wastes from factories and steel mills, plastic manufacturers and chemical processors. You take the form of phosphates, detergents, raw sewage, insecticides and herbicides that drain from the soils, acid runoff, and oil spills. Our waters absorb the heat and wastes of our industrial life, destroying marine life, killing our fellow creatures, the plants and animals of the rivers and oceans.

Now in repentant hope to restore our waters to their healthful state, we call upon you to make way for uncontaminated waters and the fresh taste of pure springs.

Hear our cry and depart, deadly spirits of pollution!

ALL SHOUT: Out, demons, out! (*drum roll, ringing bells*)

EXORCISM OF SOCIETY

CANTOR (Chanted in plain chant, holding up a piece of crushed paper or an empty tin can):

Depart deadly spirits of exploitation. We recognize you for what you are, an evergrowing threat to all life forms, to all created things. You come to us in deceptive guises, in the name of progress, science, and development. You parade in the pomp of modern skyscrapers, ever denser networks of urbanization, technology, and transportation systems. But behind the glittering façade of steel and glass lie the hovels of impoverishment and misery of the great masses of our fellow human beings. To retain your grip upon an unjust share of the resources of the earth, you threaten all life with nuclear annihilation.

Now, in repentant hope to bring our societies back to that just balance where all may share in the goods of God's Creation, we call upon you to relax your greedy and destructive grip upon our peoples and our earth; to make way for that good earth of justice and peace.

Hear our cry and depart, deadly spirits of exploitation!

ALL SHOUT: Out, demons, out! (*drum roll, ringing bells*)

CHAPTER 6

Grief and Sorrow

HEARTBROKEN • RIBS CRACKED, NOSE BROKEN

REDEMPTION AND GRACE • SERPENT'S TOOTH

OF DAUGHTERS AND A MOTHER'S HEART • A MOTHER'S HOPE

SAD, NOT ANGRY • IN THE DARK • TOO YOUNG TO BE A WIDOW

DOWN TO EIGHTY POUNDS • I DIDN'T KNOW HER WELL

TO MY BROTHER • WIFE WITHOUT WINGS

FINE • HOPE AND REDEMPTION

HEARTBROKEN

ANONYMOUS

Mothering an adolescent is painful and challenging in the best of times. My teenaged son broke the law and was arrested. Police and detectives came in and out of my home.

"Heartbroken" is the mildest description I can find for the days and months that followed. This moment defines the before and after of a mother's life. That was then, this is now. Everything is changed.

The shame is searing. I know that I committed no crime. Many church people and friends have been compassionate and steady companions along the way, believing in me. Still, as a mother, I have felt the ache and burden of responsibility. I wondered what I did wrong, what I could have done differently, what might have occurred if I had acted sooner, not acted at all, disciplined differently. Mothers I know have empathized with my grief and shame. Others have looked at me blankly. His own father has not felt a personal connection to the crime and seems not to worry about his fatherly responsibility, while I simply cannot remove it from my soul.

Still, as a mother, I have felt the ache and burden of responsibility. I wondered what I did wrong...

It might be in a mother's genetic structure to feel the weight of responsibility, albeit slightly irrational, when our child strays from the path.

The lingering questions burn in me: Trust is broken, and how shall it be repaired? When will I be able to move forward and trust him again? How will he manage to go forward from here? How do I go forward? What is right, now that everything seems wrong?

Is this how God feels when I do wrong or reject her wisdom? Does she feel responsible in some incomprehensible way? Does she lie awake at night hurting for me, crying out for shame and broken trust and worry for the relationship and for my future?

Mother Jesus, have mercy on mothers and sons.

RIBS CRACKED, NOSE BROKEN
ANONYMOUS

In the midst of the probationary months after my adolescent son's arrest, he lived for a short time with his father across town. One morning they had an argument, and his father beat him savagely. My son's face was bloody, his nose was broken, ribs cracked, bones bruised.

Apart from a child's untimely death, it was this mother's worst nightmare.

I sat by his emergency room bed crushed, wishing he were small enough to cradle tenderly. He moved between painful sobbing to cool, calculating rage, pushing me away in overwhelming vulnerability and then back to protectiveness toward me. My heart rocked swiftly, schizophrenically, between white-hot anger and piercing anguish, twisted sorrow and fear. I knew those many years ago that this man was dangerous. Why did I let my son go there?

My mind swirled from practical matters of what to do next, how to keep both of us safe and hidden, to the most satisfying revenges that I would gladly lavish upon this perpetrator father, and back to sensible conversations with doctors and detectives. I witnessed both my own strength and woeful inadequacy.

I would gladly have borne my son's pain, scooped it up on me. I wished to go back in time and make different decisions.

In God's great love, Jesus laid down his life, his comfort, his power, for generations and millennia of earthly friends. He saw our pain in all its blood and rage, in all its tender alienation and crushing vulnerability. He bore it, claimed it as his own before it destroyed us. I feel threateningly broken, but I know Jesus bears it with me. I will myself to thank him. And I ponder the unimaginable— how it would be if he had not taken it for us?

I believe, help thou mine unbelief.

REDEMPTION AND GRACE
ANGELA BOATRIGHT-SPENCER

The young man's mind and heart had given out. He hung by his fingertips from the edge of the glass wall of the hospital atrium, his feet pointing to the certain death awaiting him on the floor several stories below. His face was red, his mouth a dark, wide-open silent scream when the priest, on a routine visit, stepped out of the elevator. Her energy level was low, her prayers were dry and crackly, like leaves that skittered away in the slightest wind. She wasn't ready when the young man shouted over the heads of the police officers and hospital guards swarming around him: "Is that a priest?"

Surely, he hadn't meant her, she thought, but of course he had.

Reluctantly, she walked toward him. Her mind repeated a short version of the Jesus Prayer: "Lord Jesus, have mercy." Her heart pounded.

"What can I do for you?" she asked. Her voice was surprisingly calm and even.

"I want you to forgive me for what I'm about to do," he said, and she found herself saying, ridiculously, "And what is that?" She started talking about her son, how she comforted him when he was upset. Her son was seven, she said. He said his mother had died when he was seven. She sat cross-legged a few feet from the glass wall with her Prayer Book on her lap, its worn, gold cross gleaming in the dim light. His eyes locked on it for a moment. She continued to speak and pray, "Lord Jesus, have mercy....Jesus, Jesus…"

Time passed. A psychiatrist and the police took turns speaking to the young man. He startled everyone when, suddenly, he drew his legs up and, in one perfect motion, catapulted himself over the wall. He landed with his face on the Prayer Book. On the worn golden cross, he placed one single kiss. After a moment, the police pulled him up and took him away.

> *O ruler of the universe, Lord God, great deeds are they*
> *that you have done, surpassing human understanding.*
>
> —"THE SONG OF THE REDEEMED,"
> THE BOOK OF COMMON PRAYER

This meditation is based on an actual event originally described in the book, *In the Time of Trouble,* published by LeaderResources and written by Angela Boatright. ©1993-2002, Angela Boatright.

SERPENT'S TOOTH

FLORENCE KREJCI

First child of my body,
Child of my heart—far, far away
Not only in miles but in affection.
Why?
What can I do to bring her closer
When she does not want closer?
Our children are but lent from You,
The One who creates them.
But I never wished it to be bitter loss
When she grew and went.
You made her to love and to be loved,
and indeed, she is greatly loved.
But she is not loving.
Oh, bitter, bitter serpent's tooth!
God grant that I may open empty hands
And let her fly free of my longing!

OF DAUGHTERS AND A MOTHER'S HEART

KAY COLLIER MCLAUGHLIN

My stepdaughter died today—from a massive, shocking heart attack at just-turned forty.

"Step" is the official descriptor of who we were to each other, but it doesn't begin to touch the relationship itself. The definition I carry with me happened in a department store in California when we were shopping for a dress she would wear to her cousin's wedding.

"Your mother is welcome to join you in the dressing room," the clerk chirped cheerily.

My "daughter" grinned mischievously and held the door open. "You're my 'friend-mother,'" she said, "so it's okay."

Whether sitting on the back porch or at the kitchen table, I felt God's hand in this divine mix.

A hyphenated quickstep around one of the most precious and emotionally complex relationships in the world: mother and daughter.

It seems to me that when God made the mother's heart, he made it expandable, capable of holding an infinite number of "children" over a lifetime. I am blessed with daughters of the spirit, whose life stories intertwine with mine in deep and mysterious ways that enrich us both.

When my own daughters were growing up, our house was a gathering place for their peers, whose joys and sorrows mingled with those of our family as naturally as the stray jeans or socks found their way into the family wash. Conversations long into the night were a norm. The only caveat was that each young person understand that while they were sitting in my living room talking about their lives—including their parents—my own daughters were hopefully finding a safe place elsewhere to do the same. That was big news to my young friends, who had yet to reach the place in life where they recognized the need to separate and surrogate before they could come home again. But God knew. Whether sitting on the back porch or at the kitchen table, I felt God's hand in this divine mix.

They had their own names for me. "Mama Kay." "Nother Mother." Titles are not only inadequate, but inconsequential. It's as futile as trying to catch a falling star.

My stepdaughter's death is a poignant reminder of all the daughters of my heart—and the mystery and power of human connection.

Carried not under my heart—but in it.

A MOTHER'S HOPE
SALLY M. BROWER

Your heartbeat could never be heard.
But from your first appearing,
    a tiny shadow of being
    outlined on the luminous arcing embrace
    of welcoming womb,
    I rejoiced at your creation.

I did not know I could love so completely
    one so unformed, uncertain, yet
    clinging fiercely,
    growing in the dark hallowed depths
    of a mother's hope.
I prayed for your preservation.

You were not created for a life on earth.
You ceased to grow,
    but even then,
    ending your existence
    was never a choice.
I pleaded for God's intervention.

So much blood lost, so much grief spilled;
    the hull of my heart so emptied out
        and yet so full of God.

SAD, NOT ANGRY
WANDA RUTH COPELAND

Even my bishop said it: "You probably are angry with God."

No, I'm not. How can I be angry? I have just spent twenty-five years of my life with Tom, the best man in the world. He was gentle and kind, sensitive and honest. He was fun, universally loved, and he chose to spend the last years of that life with me. Angry? No, not at all.

I am so grateful to our loving God who gave me the chance to be loved by such an amazing man. I had no idea that two people could be so well-suited for each other. Like peanut butter and jelly; like two pieces of sandwich meat when we slept. We just made sense going through life together.

How can I be angry with a God who has blessed me so much? Tom is the one who mentored me from my (emotionally) late adolescence into the fullness of my own womanhood. I was twenty-seven when we met. Looking back, I was incredibly naïve and sheltered. Tom taught me self-awareness and introduced me to my own power and wisdom. He taught me to laugh, and to cry unabashedly.

Angry at his death? No. I'm not angry, I'm fiercely sad. Why do I want to continue without him? I feel disconnected from what I've come to know. It's not that I can't go on with life. It's that it's tedious to try to find the strength to meet another day. It's that some days I don't see why I should. With Tom I had the best life that I could have ever imagined for myself.

God, help me imagine what's next.

IN THE DARK

JOY NIMNOM KRAUS

In the dark
I talk to God.
I listen for answers
that never come.
I speak my fear.
I ask for help
I don't receive.
I drift upon a raft
of a belief I don't believe.
I bump among the reeds of *No*.
And sleep.

. . . .

I will have nothing to do with a God who cares only occasionally.
I need a God who is with us always, everywhere,
in the deepest depths as well as the highest heights.
It is when things go wrong, when good things do not happen,
when our prayers seem to have been lost, that God is most present.
We do not need the sheltering wings when things go smoothly.
We are closest to God in the darkness, stumbling along blindly.
—MADELEINE L'ENGLE

TOO YOUNG TO BE A WIDOW
WANDA RUTH COPELAND

Widows are supposed to be old. They have nicely coifed grey hair because they go to the beauty shop every Friday. They have slightly gnarled fingers or walk with a slower gait. They saw it coming, because that's what you expect after forty or fifty years together. You just know that it's going to happen. And it does. It's to be expected. Ah, expectations.

What about the expectation that together we would see grandchildren graduate from high school? What about the expectation that retirement is something we would slide into gradually? What about being together long enough that I could look forward to not having you around for a day?

I'm too young to be a widow.

Help me, God.

DOWN TO EIGHTY POUNDS
CORALIE VOCE HAMBLETON

I walk out of the nursing center after visiting my mother. Ninety-six, she fell last spring causing spinal stress fractures that made it impossible for her to remain at home—the home in which she'd been born, where she'd lived independently since my father died thirty-four years ago. Always self-reliant, she now relies on staff for everything from toileting to rolling over in bed.

The Thanksgiving after my father died, Mom fell as well—breaking a hip, requiring two major surgeries, leaving her vulnerable to crippling curvature of the spine and pain. But she'd borne it.

Now, down to eighty pounds with her body so twisted she lists to one side when sitting up, she's ready to die. Her vision and hearing nearly gone, she wishes she could just take a pill and slip from this life into Jesus' heavenly hands.

I understand. I'd feel the same way. Still alert, she's in pain, knows she won't improve, and feels she's lived out her purpose. She doesn't even have the strength to hold her infant great-grandson.

Why is it so hard to die?

I suffer with her. I don't do helplessness well. I'm a take-action kind of person. But this requires waiting and accepting that there is nothing I can do to make her suffering easier—except to be present, to listen, to be patient, and to pray with her. And to realize that her increasing demands and irritation arise from her frustration at no longer having any control over her living or her dying.

I am grateful for faith. Hers, knowing that she has always walked with the Lord and is confident she will rest eternally in heaven; mine, that assures me that I walk this painfully slow, agonizing journey with Christ at my side. He's familiar with agonizing waiting, too. Even in this grief, God will show both Mom and me his strength and presence in ways we can't begin to know now.

"I know, Mom, I'm so sorry that you're hurting, but God is still teaching us something important. I love you, Mom."

I DIDN'T KNOW HER WELL
NANCY R. DUVALL

I didn't know her well enough.
She was thirty-six and I was ten
    when she died. My brother
    was six months old.

He might be the lucky one.
He has no memories lurking
    in the corners of his mind,
    connecting, then flittering
    almost away
    as I try to grab hold of one.

My most vivid memories are sitting
    in her lap, listening to a story
    and sucking my thumb as I
    ran my fingers over her
      silk blouse.
Heaven—books and all that love!

I also remember dropping a pot
on her arch and seeing her cry
    for the first and only time.
I was in awe. I did not know
    she could hurt like that.

I didn't know the half of it.
When I dropped the pot
    on her foot, she was pregnant
    with my brother, while battling
    a cancerous brain tumor
affecting her sight and balance.

How I wish I could know her now.
    I would hold her on my lap
and read her the sweetest books
while I hug her tight and tell her
    how much I have missed her.

TO MY BROTHER
ANONYMOUS

It's been a long time since I spoke with you or saw you. But I need to say some things.

I hated you. I hated your coldness, your derision, and your lack of compassion. You just couldn't or wouldn't be warm. You withheld love and you hated me in such a personal way. It was so clear you thought that I—*me*—very

I hated you.
I hated your
coldness, your derision, and
your lack of compassion.

personally deserved to be hated. You found me so annoying and irritating. And I didn't know how not to be. You attacked, but you did not instruct. I couldn't even change to be more likeable because I didn't know how and I didn't have the will.

I hated you for making me feel so awful, so like I'd earned your hatred by just being me. It was being me that earned this pain. I hated you and I hated me. You made me want to die.

I can analyze it all now, acknowledge that we had no parent capable of correcting the harmful thinking and actions on both our parts. You were sick and I was sick and we blamed each other. But that analysis doesn't heal.

I truly don't know what I ever did to you to make you hate me so much. And you died before we could ever talk about it.

I'd like to say I'm sorry for all my retaliatory actions and all my annoying ways, but I don't really feel that. They were all I had to defend against you. But what I am sorry about is that we couldn't be friends. I'm sorry your heart was so closed. I'm sorry you couldn't love. I'm sorry you had to take a gun and shoot yourself.

We are the same, you and I. So separated from our innocence, from love, and so angry about it. I've never really regretted my actions or omissions toward you.

I've never taken that guilt on myself. Whatever I did or didn't do are just the sterile facts. But I regret I couldn't love you. I regret being so sick I couldn't see your sickness. I could only see your meanness.

I regret hating you so much. I regret not understanding that you were dying of poison—of the absence of love—of the twisting and warping of love. I regret not understanding that even in your cruelty you were as powerless as I was, and for the same reason: we were separated from love and from help.

I've gotten the help, but I'm still separated from love.

To forgive you would be arrogant because you couldn't help it.

So I ask this instead: *God, please help me to release my brother into the love he never had here. To release all bitterness in my heart and to retain only love for my absent brother, whom I miss.*

··

*The soul that would preserve its peace, when another's sin is brought to mind,
must fly from it as from the pains of hell, looking to God for help against it.
To consider the sins of other people will produce a thick film over the eyes of our soul,
and prevent us for the time being from seeing the "fair beauty of the Lord"—
unless, that is, we look at the sins contrite along with the sinner,
being sorry with and for him, and yearning over him for God.*

—JULIAN OF NORWICH

WIFE WITHOUT WINGS
TARA LYLE

Be angry but do not sin;
do not let the sun go down on your anger.
—EPHESIANS 4:26

Imagine in the wee hours of the night witnessing someone clinging spread-eagle on the hood of a moving car. Would that be too much to believe? Would you think it was only a figment of your imagination? After all, who goes around (other than superheroes) clinging to the hoods of cars?

Maybe you are not able to conjure up such an image. That very episode happened during the early years of my marriage. It would be one of many chaotic times that ensued. That incident was a representation of how out of control my life and marriage were.

I was in my early twenties, and I thought I could prevent my husband from leaving the house after we had argued. I didn't have enough insight to realize that no two people solved problems identically. I preferred to sit down and talk; my husband preferred to take flight. Balance was missing from our marriage. In our early years, God was not at the apex even though I maintained a relationship with him. I was more vested in building up my marriage than in allowing God to be the head. I always believed in God, but I felt unworthy of his encompassing love for so many years.

My church was a tremendous support, but I did not allow people there to see the depths of my pain.

As I sit in prison for killing my husband, I sometimes reflect on all the things that went wrong during our thirteen-year marriage. I suffered emotional, verbal, and physical abuse, and I protected that secret for a long time. We relied more on ourselves to fix things in the marriage, and that was a sure recipe for disaster.

My church was a tremendous support, but I did not allow people there to see the depths of my pain. I had loving sisters and great friends who would have given their full support if only I had shared what was going on within my marriage.

I'm convinced if I had allowed others into my world and embraced help, I wouldn't be incarcerated today. I encourage anyone facing any type of abuse to share your personal turmoil with another person. Don't remain silent; seek help. I was paralyzed by my silence. There were so many people who would have helped me if I had only given voice to my suffering.

Does the story end there? No. Whatever transgressions occur in your life, your choice to move beyond the fall is yours. My motto is: My transgression doesn't define the person I am or the person I will grow to be in Christ.

I know for sure the only wings I will ever have are the ones rooted in the Word.

FINE

ELIZABETH BUENING

> *For had it been an adversary who taunted me,*
> *then I could have borne it…*
> *But it was you, a man after my own heart,*
> *my companion, my own familiar friend.*
> —PSALM 55:13-14

"Fine" is one of the most misused words in a woman's vocabulary. We use it when we give in or want to end an argument: *It's fine—let's just eat where you want.* In thinly veiled annoyance and anger: *Don't worry about spilling coffee on the report, it's fine.* We use it to lie: *I'm fine.*

In college I spent an afternoon dissecting the many uses of the word "fine" with my best guy friend. Let's call him Aaron. The overlying hypothesis of the joking-but-serious conversation was that when a woman says "fine" in response to something a man has said, he's done something wrong.

Five months later I stood in the doorway of Aaron's room and said to him, "It's fine. I'm fine," before turning toward the elevators to leave late one Friday night. In under an hour my most trusted guy friend had become my rapist. And now he was too tired to walk me out. And I was fine.

Except that I wasn't, of course. I was confused and angry and too horrified to name what he'd done to me. So I jumped straight into denial: I must have misunderstood what happened. Aaron would never hurt me like that. And so on…

Even when he apologized the next day for "being out of control," I couldn't name it. I kept thinking that if we started dating, what he did wouldn't have to count because being intimate would be part of our relationship, not a violation of our friendship. It wouldn't hurt me. It would be fine. But you can't cancel out rape retroactively.

He disgusted me, but I tried to stay friends—because I was fine. It took me two and a half years to name what he'd done. Two and a half years of telling myself that no man would ever love me, that I was nothing. The anger I'd held down surged and I cut him out of my life. I felt empowered but also victimized.

In a therapy group for survivors I heard my story in theirs, felt the collective pain we were in. But most importantly, they understood what happened to me. And said it mattered. Which is a gift I thank God for every day. My own choir of angels, and they were just like me.

For he shall give his angels charge over you,
to keep you in all your ways.
—PSALM 91:11

HOPE AND REDEMPTION

ANONYMOUS

Many of us are survivors. We are your mothers, your sisters, your best friends, your coworkers. For me, adopted into a family stricken with mental illness, it was a childhood filled with physical, sexual, and emotional abuse. I don't remember a time before the trauma, even from early childhood. I remember running around the house as fast as I could to escape my mother's uncontrollable rage, only to give up and let her catch me, absorbing the blows from the belt until her fury was spent.

I remember being left alone with her sick and violent brother and his

I don't know how I survived. At times I thought I would die.

son, and the horrible things that followed. I remember walking home from the bus stop after school, my steps getting slower and slower as I got closer to home, a knot of fear in my gut so big I could hardly breathe.

I don't know how I survived. At times I thought I would die. But I didn't. I know that God was with me, sustaining me, carrying me when I couldn't put one foot in front of the other, when I couldn't see a way through the darkness. Eventually the truth came out, at least some of it. I wasn't the only victim. Some of us survived. In time, the Lord brought healing. Kind and courageous people were willing to walk the path with me. God did the impossible in my life.

I have a wonderful husband, children, and grandchildren. Out of the terrible came a knowledge of God's redeeming power and love, for "all things work together for good for those who love God, who are called according to his purpose....in all these things we are more than conquerors through him who loved us" (Romans 8:28, 37).

CHAPTER

Lessons of the Heart

SWEDISH COFFEE AND A YOUNG SAINT

DEVON ANDERSON

As the first-born girl in my Swedish family, the mantle of Santa Lucia was mine. This honor meant getting up before dawn every December thirteenth—the feast day for Lucia—assembling the breakfast tray of steaming Swedish coffee and saffron buns, donning my Lucia garb (white robe, red sash, garland of holly) and waking up each member of the family. I loved opening the doors to the silent bedrooms, pitch dark except for the shadows cast by my small candle. I loved being the only one awake and bringing the light into each room. And then it was the slow-moving process of people waking up, turning on lights, whispering, coming downstairs to the breakfast table. It was like watching a wave wash over the house, gently transforming it from quiet and dark to alive and light.

I loved being the only one awake and bringing the light into each room.

Lucia, whose name means "light," was thought to have lived in Sicily around 300 A.D. Tradition says that she had a strong Christian faith and openly proclaimed it by distributing all her earthly belongings to the poor. But Lucia, though deeply devout and faithful, had a defiant streak and was eventually denounced and sentenced to death. She died on the winter solstice. Lucia's day became observed in Scandinavia where winter festivals were held annually to greet the lengthening of days and the return of light. Legends say that during a famine in Sweden, Santa Lucia, her head surrounded by light, miraculously appeared and provided the country with food.

I am grown now and have a first-born daughter of my own. Every December thirteenth she humors me, straps on the Santa Lucia gown and carries her little candle into our dark bedrooms. The feast of Lucia reminds me, each year, of the power of light as a symbol for God's unceasing, faithful presence. It reminds me that there is no corner, no crevice, no hard-edged unforgiving darkness in all our lives that is not—thanks be to God—vulnerable to hope and transformation.

UNEXPECTED BLESSINGS
NOËL ALHBUM BAILEY

I felt like "the little old woman who lived in a shoe" that was crowded with children. I had opened my home, the parish rectory, for immigrants who were flooding into the Berkshires of western Massachusetts. First was a neighbor whose husband had hit her; she was in a shelter and hating it. I gave her shelter until home was safe again, and she was the inspiration for starting Spanish language worship.

Next was a family from Ecuador: mother, father, and two teenaged daughters. Their son was staying with relatives. I sat with them on the evening of 9/11 as we all tried to fathom what was happening to this country that they had come to as a safe haven.

When the first day of school came, Monica was ready to set off by herself— her parents had gone to work. (They left behind in Ecuador a medical clinic in which they were both doctors, but could find work only as orderlies here.) I'm not very good at walking into new situations, and Monica looked like a scared rabbit. We hugged and cried a bit, and then I scrounged up a notebook and some paper and pencils and sent her off with a kiss and a prayer.

Then came Maria and, in a few months, her son Jeffrey Moises. My "shoe" had fewer people, but the year Jeffrey was with me it was filled with exuberant life. Then came Paul, recovering from surgery, followed by his parents from Colombia. They shared a room, and together we nursed Paul through chemo and back to health.

We have shared God's love in worship, baptisms, weddings—and in being together with and for each other. God's blessings come in many forms, sometimes even before we open—or shut—our doors.

If you can't feed one hundred people,
then feed just one.
—MOTHER TERESA

DIRT BETWEEN MY FINGERS
NANCY HOPKINS-GREENE

May is always a challenging month. With end-of-year activities—sports events, church meetings and celebrations, concerts and recitals—my calendar is full. There is no time for spring cleaning, and my house is a mess. My southern Ohio garden starts to look like a jungle. Truth is, my garden and my household become icons for my life: overgrown, invaded, and overwhelmed.

First, there are the weeds that need pulling: concerns and burdens that I need to let go of and put into the compost pile. Sometimes I just need to uproot that weedy idea that I can do everything, or that it is all up to me. But weeds aren't the only problem: my life becomes overgrown, invaded, and overwhelmed with many good things, like my strawberry plants and raspberry canes.

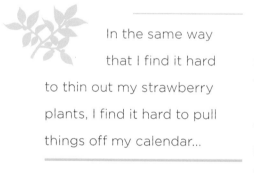

And then I think of Jesus' words: "I am the true vine, and my Father is the vinegrower. He removes every branch in me that bears no fruit. Every branch that bears fruit he prunes to make it bear more fruit" (John 15:1-2).

Sometimes my life needs some pruning. In the same way that I find it hard to thin out my strawberry plants, I find it hard to pull things off my calendar, to say no to the next great mission project idea or the next friend who wants to go out for lunch.

> In the same way that I find it hard to thin out my strawberry plants, I find it hard to pull things off my calendar...

Sometimes I simply need to live with and accept the overabundance. Other times I need to weed and prune.

I have no great words of wisdom or advice on how to live with overgrown lives. But as I go out to my garden in the spring, I try to be present: to hear the birds, to feel the dirt between my fingers, to do one thing at a time. I remind myself that I can only do so much, that less can be more, and that there can be too much of a good thing.

My beloved daughter
Ruth Lawson Kirk

Often the first response upon meeting someone is to speak of an occupation or vocation. Yet we are more than what we do. The Good News proclaims one's identity.

"Who are you?"

Who I am is dependent on my connections with others: "I am a wife and mother." "I am rector of Christ Church Christiana Hundred in Wilmington, Delaware."

But when a crisis, such as unemployment, damages our relationships, the devastation can be huge for the person whose sense of self comes solely from these roles.

"Who are you?"

Like the rest of the universe, we are the products of God's design and we are marvelous, wondrous creations. The Good News proclaims we are God's beloved children. We are daughters created in God's image—born and born again in baptism to have the grace we need to magnify the fullness of God within. God's love is energizing life in us, just as in Jesus, when the crowds on the riverbank heard the voice proclaim, "You are my Son, the beloved; with you I am well pleased" (Mark 1:11).

"Who are you?"

We are so much more than what we do for a living, or who we are bound to by blood or vow, or even the image we criticize in front of the mirror. Listen carefully to the Author of Life, the only one who can name our truest nature and identity. God is saying to you and me, "My beloved daughter." These are the first words that define you. What will be different about our life stories when we truly believe them?

PONDERING
CAMILLE HEGG

Mary treasured all these words and
pondered them in her heart.
—LUKE 2:19

Mary, the mother of Jesus, pondered the things that happened and were said to her at the birth of her baby. That verse has always captured my imagination. I look at the stars and the moon and I think and wonder. On my best days, I see a flower and marvel. I hold a new baby and am filled with emotion, gratitude.

When my own baby was born, I stared at the miracle she was. I pondered—and I knew something of Mary and of other mothers through the ages. I learned to ponder from Mary.

She took into her heart God, who had taken up residence in her. She pondered what was being asked of her. She allowed God to grow in her and change her for life. Making a space for the Spirit and her baby within her heart, she did not run away. She pondered right down into the ambiguities of life.

The root of "ponder" comes from "weigh." And pondering happens when we weigh something—through thought, speech, silence—allowing that something to take root within us. It is not always cozy and comfortable. It can be vigorous and daring, but it can lead, as it did for Mary, to new awareness of the depths and mysteries of life.

On a personal level, we might be reluctant to ponder our life choices, assuming that some choices, having been made, are beyond changing; but as with Mary there may be more possibilities before us than we at first imagined.

Our pondering can be the umbilical cord that connects us to nourishing, creative, whole, and holy responses to life.

COME, LORD CHRIST
BITSY AYRES RUBSAMEN

Endless stories,

jabberings

are born of man's ego.

They are penned

fruitlessly.

Never ending,

ever weaving,

ever dancing wide circles around

the Truth.

Unbalanced,

wavering,

they teeter on the edge

of what is Real

and yet they

do not speak

the power of Your

Love

to the human heart.

Come, Lord Christ.

Break through the darkness.

Enlighten

the woman who

seeks

to weave tales of fantasy and desire.

Tell us *your* story!

SEEKING SOPHIA

ERIN MARTINEAU

In a time and a place when calculation and plans reign, how can I learn to listen for that quiet whisper of wisdom? To sense the breath of our ancestors? To feel the leaping of my very cells?

The woods call to me, but too often I resist, saying, "Just one more thing, let me finish this one last thing." But that to-do list never ends: pay the bills, buy insurance against the future, count the calories, and respond to the email. Build a fortress against all my fears and worries, make sure the coming years will be secure. Make sure I'm not going off the deep end, out into the wilds, alone.

But all of Creation beckons. And when I'm deep-down quiet, I can feel the others there with me. I walk through the leaves; I enter the grove; I lie in the grass; the frenetic falls away. We abide there, together, and I begin to remember.

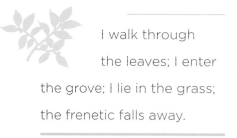

I walk through the leaves; I enter the grove; I lie in the grass; the frenetic falls away.

I remember we are all kin, all of us who are on this tiny luminous ball. I remember that we are spinning in the blackest of seas, with the thinnest of veils that allow us to breathe.

All of Creation beckons me, asks me to push away from the desk, to step away from the computer screen, to open myself to the mystery, to take up the rhythm of life itself, ever evolving, without a plan, no calculator in hand. To reawaken, with arms outstretched.

The greatest challenge of the day is:
how to bring about a revolution of the heart.
—DOROTHY DAY

WITNESS

MARGARET ROSE

Whenever I read of new violence in the Congo—thirty women raped, children kidnapped for soldiers, a village burned—the words leap off the page and I think of my friend Mugisa who lives there. Her own husband was kidnapped and thankfully returned unharmed. Her house was robbed. She experienced the horrors of women dying from multiple rapes and fistulas caused by pregnancy, friends murdered while their children were forced to watch.

> She has a dream and a vision that will not let her go.

I wonder, when Mugisa tells me these stories, why she is not bitter, why she is not so angry that her only action would be to fight back at those who have done this to her country, her friends, her family. Yet, what she has seen and her steadfast faith have only spurred her to healing action. She has started an education and empowerment project for the women of her region. She is unrelenting in her quest for new opportunities for the women who have been brutalized to find their own voices. And she seeks in every possible corner for funds to fulfill this dream.

Perhaps that is it. She has a dream and a vision that will not let her go. That passion gives her strength and courage and is fueled by a conviction that God's desire for Creation is joy and wonder, goodness and wholeness for all people.

What a witness Mugisa is for me when petty injustices make me want to lash out or get even! I pray for my own faith to give me strength and courage to follow in Mugisa's way—to make no peace with injustice yet to persist in peacemaking and the empowerment of those around me. And not to lose hope.

A MYSTIC'S POLAR BEAR
JUDITH HOLLOWAY BAUM

With trav'lers of experience, I was willing to go
to regions low within my heart
where you dwell, Lord.

Led by the voice, gentle and knowing, I followed in prayer
to a point where the path narrowed.
My choice was gone.

Coming closer now, your presence felt, I approached the bend
and the end of my search for you.
A polar bear?

What does this mean? A symbol or sign? Oh! I fear to think
Of bears extinct—or universe
killed—by my greed.

Pondering thoughts too dark to sort out, I grasp for refuge
but am deluged by mystery...
Ah! I'm in you.

MOTHER-IN-LAW
LYNN FAIRFIELD

He stood over her and rebuked the fever, and it left her.
Immediately she got up and began to serve them.
—LUKE 4:39

Her fever breaking—anyone might ail—
Inaugurates his practice; ribbon cut
And he is besieged. She isn't named but
We know what her relationships entail.
A woman chosen, like the Virgin, so we'd
See her healed body standing frail
With eager energy to make the meal:
The sonless widow's joy to serve and feed.
This all takes place one Sabbath, day of rules;
The sick, the poor don't notice rubrics much.
The widow's fever—high, Luke says—then cools
With Jesus' Sabbath-breaking touch.
If healing cracks the codes men make,
Perhaps those rules were meant to break.

RUTH AND NAOMI

CATHY H. GEORGE

I love this story about women and our loyalty to each other. I love that it is about a daughter-in-law devoted to her mother-in-law, a relationship often considered competitive or conflictual. Ruth, a Moabite, marries the widow Naomi's son, and when he dies, both women are left with no security. They set off for Judah, Naomi's homeland, but Naomi tells Ruth to return to her own mother, her own people. No obligation but love causes Ruth to say to Naomi, "Your people shall be my people, and your God my God" (Ruth 1:1-17).

> We are sisters, we share each other's burdens and know each other's trials.

My first husband's mother introduced me to the Episcopal Church. She believed in me, she encouraged me. When our marriage was ending she did what she had promised to do: "all in her power to support us" in our marriage. It didn't go the way she wanted, or the way either of us hoped. Beyond the years of marriage to her son, however, she still believed in me and encouraged me as a mother in faith.

When I was in Jerusalem, I stayed at St. George's College. In the morning on my walk I saw Muslim women in head scarves and long dresses walking arm in arm. They traveled the sidewalk close to each other, their faces in intimate contact as they held onto each other, sharing the care of the children who ran ahead or lagged behind. In the marketplace, they held up scarves against each other's faces and laughed as they filled baskets with dates, nuts, rice, and vegetables. They had a life of their own that a man did not enter.

Women are often pitted against each other, taught to compete, thought of as rivals. But we are not. We are sisters, we share each other's burdens and know each other's trials. We deserve and need one another, arm in arm. There is something powerful about women looking out for women.

Chasing away devils of self-doubt

Lee Krug

I grew up in an era when girls played with dolls, girls did not play with boys, and grown women were wise to defer to grown men.

My mother, however, taught me that I could do anything I wanted to do—yes, even be President. A feminist before the word was popular, I searched out the Jesus who included and affirmed women as his followers. Although the culture was still an influence, my little dog—a tiny blond Chihuahua named Jason—helped me stay confident.

He was only three inches long when we brought him home; it was terrible to contemplate anyone stepping on him. A feisty and loveable pet, he was territorial and protective. Fiercely he would go—with many yaps—after the Doberman, the Rottweiler, and the Great Dane who dared to come into our yard, making them run for their lives. His philosophy: God had made him a Chihuahua, and therefore he could do anything he perceived as his right or duty.

What a lesson in self-esteem! Apparently it never occurred to him that he would be one mouthful for these giant dogs, and it never occurred to them that he couldn't eat them alive. Amused, I watched him, almost unaware that he was teaching me that my limitations were in my own head.

I think God has turned Jason loose in his heavenly kingdom to chase away the devils of self-doubt. And, although imperfectly, I am finding that being female (as Jason was small) does not define or limit me, either.

> *To be able to say* YES *to yourself when all the environment is shouting* NO,
> *but to be able to listen to that* NO *and hear what message*
> *it is sending from which you can profit—in my experience,*
> *that is certainly beyond the possibility of fragile human beings.*
> *That takes a leap of faith. That takes a religious dimension.*
>
> —Verna Dozier

The love child of Holy Mother Wisdom
Sally M. Brower

I will live as the love child of Holy Mother Wisdom;
sailing with her through the white sky of morning
into the mystery of light unknown, abandoning all
for the sake of the Great Love who gave me birth.

I will live as the golden child who has been promised a kingdom,
soaring up to the heights of heaven and scaling the precipices
of my own love-cleft heart, risking all that I am
for the sake of the Deep Love who calls me home.

I will live as the child created just now,
ever new progeny of the greening power of God,
always seeking for signs of the true Life,
searching verdant pastures and green-mossed mountains,
spending all that I have
for the sake of the Gift Love who births life through me.

I will live as a passionate child of the wild places;
dweller of ruby borderlands,
fearless traverser of garnet thresholds,
wayfarer of the red-flamed wilderness; waiting, yearning,
for the sake of the Ever Love who woos my wounded heart
and heals my wandering soul.

GRACE IS MY RIVER
NANCY R. DUVALL

Grace is my river.
It flows through my life,
    sometimes slowly,
    sometimes overwhelming
        in its nourishing floods.

It takes me around jagged rocks of
    death and disappointment,
    missed opportunities and what ifs,
and far more often my river

    holds waters of comfort for my soul.
Its cleansing tides of love and faith
    move me through the shallows
    of self-doubt and self-pity.

Grace is my river.
It flows through my life.
When my frail boat of faith fails me
I ask Grace to enfold me with
    its warm embrace.

O Grace, carry me, carry me on
    in the arms of Jesus
    to the throne of God.

TWOGETHER
LEE KRUG

In the Book of Genesis we find God providing Eve as a mate for Adam, so that he would not be lonely. It was God's own loneliness that led him to create the world and its creatures, especially human beings. Today's woman is likely to question the idea that she has been brought into the world to assuage a mate's need for a companion. Jesus shows us how God values women and their needs in their own right.

However, in the first swoon of falling in love, a woman may not ask any guidance from the Holy Spirit of life and love. She idealizes her beloved and, even with the advantage of premarital counseling, she (and he) will remain besotted with the other. What attracts you to your mate often turns out, after marriage or a sacred commitment, to be the very quality that drives you crazy.

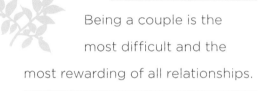

Being a couple is the most difficult and the most rewarding of all relationships.

A strong, confident male changes, in his partner's eyes, into a controlling complainer. Since this works both ways, a vivacious woman may later seem to have turned into a prickly over-talker. Have they changed? Did both deny, in their desire for a perfect other, the all too human flaws in each of them?

Being a couple is the most difficult and the most rewarding of all relationships. The hardest part of living with another person is to allow your partner to be who he or she is. "Different is beautiful; God bless variety" was a sign in one of our churches. It was meant to be inclusive and welcoming. It could be a good model for couples. A wife might model an attitude for her husband by thinking: *You are different from me, not better nor worse. I would like you to do things exactly the way I do them, but the price of loving you is accepting that you may do them another way.*

Remember that God always has compassion. At your angriest and most alienated, search for that compassion which can lead you back to what you loved about the person in your beginnings.

WEDDING DRESS
CAROL McCREA

> *But when the king came in to see the guests,*
> *he noticed a man there who was not wearing*
> *a wedding robe, and he said to him, "Friend, how*
> *did you get in here without a wedding robe?"*
> —MATTHEW 22:11-12

How carefully we dress for a wedding—our own or someone else's: the right dress, shoes, handbag, bra (whose straps won't slip out). Hair washed and styled, perhaps even colored. No holes in stockings. Shoes to match exactly and perhaps glitter. Jewelry. Makeup, even if we don't usually wear it. Those who have husbands or boyfriends may suggest they wear certain ties, even jackets for the occasion. This is how we dress for a wedding on earth.

Jesus, so wise. You gave us an example of when people dress themselves to the teeth. (We may even bleach these for the wedding.) You attended weddings yourself (perhaps dragged by your mother, who may have insisted that you wear your best robe and clean your sandals). You knew that people prepare for weddings more than for any other event.

So what are you telling us, Jesus, about preparation for eternal life, by using our wedding example? The message is not "Come as you are." You are telling us, Lord, that our job is to prepare ourselves, to adorn our souls in their finest, to rid ourselves of spiritual rags.

We know we can stop sinning only through God's grace and Jesus' blood, but that doesn't mean we throw up our hands, saying like Popeye, "I am what I am." There is spiritual cleaning to be done, and harm to ourselves and others that needs to stop. There are daily disciplines and spiritual connections that will make us "gorgeously arrayed." This is our part of the work—dressing for eternal life. We may need help to do it: ministers, priests, church activities, retreats, spiritual reading, therapy, and self-help groups—whatever it takes. Let us prepare ourselves well for the Wedding Feast.

THINGS MY MOTHER FORGOT TO TELL ME
WESTINA MATTHEWS

Your feet get bigger. Did you know that? I didn't, until this past summer when I finally confessed to myself that that my size 7 shoes were too tight and that I needed to move up to a size 7½. One day in passing, I mentioned this to my mother. And she said, ever so casually, "Oh, didn't I tell you that? As you get older, your feet get bigger."

My mother also forgot to tell me so many other things. Like how many different kinds of tears there are...sweet tears, salty tears, bitter tears, and tearless tears. And laughter...the laughter at, the laughter for, the laughter with, and the deep, down-in-the-belly laughter that happens sometimes when I am by myself.

She forgot to tell me how hard I would cry when *he* left me, and then when *he* left me, and then when *he* left me. She also forgot to tell me how hard I would laugh, years later, about the time when *he* left me, and then *he* left me—and then "Thank you Jesus!" when *he* left me.

But there's one thing that she didn't forget to tell me, and for this I will be eternally grateful. She remembered to tell me to pray.

So, thank you, God, for walking with me through the valleys and carrying me over the mountains. Thank you, God, for mothers and grandmothers, aunts and sisters, and girlfriends who have—in their own special ways—taught me how to love, to never give up on myself, to always look up, and to never look back. And especially, God, I thank you for having the vision of what it is to be...a woman.

> She forgot to tell me how hard I would cry when *he* left me, and then when *he* left me, and then when *he* left me.

A WOMAN FULLY GROWN
WESTINA MATTHEWS

What does it feel like to be a woman…fully grown?

Because each of us is a woman…fully grown.

False starts in our twenties

shaky ground in our thirties

terra firma in our forties

quiet strength in our fifties

serenity in our sixties

wisdom in our seventies

prophets in our eighties

goddesses in our nineties.

And, if we are blessed to live as long as those two ol' Delany sisters,

Sadie and Bessie (God rest their souls), we will even "have our say"!

Yes, isn't it wonderful to be a woman…fully grown.

We have shared and survived

illness, loss of loved ones, marriages,

births, grandchildren, divorces, career changes,

hot flashes, broken promises,

dreams unfulfilled,

spiritual reawakenings, and hopes renewed.

Gentle hands

have brushed away our tears, tender hearts have forgiven our "I told you so's,"

and open arms have embraced our joys.

All daughters of the Holy One, blessed by the presence of the Divine.

We are smart. We are strong. We are bold. We are brave. We are triumphant.

We are women…fully grown.

TUESDAY'S CHILD
NOËL JULNES-DEHNER

Born on a Thursday, I fit the nursery rhyme that declares, "Thursday's child has far to go." I am on a journey, always struggling, never arriving. But today is Tuesday and I've decided to switch to "Tuesday's child is full of grace" or thankfulness.

Last week I found a wonderful birthday present for a dear friend. I was so caught up in picturing her happy face that I failed to see a mailbox and backed into it. I fumed about my accident with its repercussions and replayed the motion incessantly, as if I could change it into not having happened.

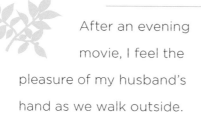

After an evening movie, I feel the pleasure of my husband's hand as we walk outside.

Full of grace today as I awake, I choose to shift the focus of my memory from the broken mailbox to how pleased my friend was. Continuing, I open the pages of my inner photo album and relive putting my arms around my daughters when they were toddlers and saying, "This is heaven."

I accept that the course of physical therapy for my already injured shoulder will now be longer because of the accident. When I watch the man next to me grimace during his session, I pray for him. When my session is painful, I pray for endurance. I give thanks for the therapist and her skill. Driving home, I take the back road and admire the trees lush with summer green. I inhale the fragrant moisture mixed with leaves and soil.

After an evening movie, I feel the pleasure of my husband's hand as we walk outside. "I'm glad we found each other," I tell him.

"The grace of the Lord Jesus be with you" (1 Corinthians 16:23). Choose grace today and send it on to others. Makes a day great.

SISTER LOVE

KAY COLLIER McLAUGHLIN

It must have started with being the middle of three sisters—but again, that kind of sibling experience could lead *away* from girl friends, before cautiously revisiting the whole idea later.

If sibling female stuff didn't cast a shadow over female relationships and point toward the *real* kind of love in life (romantic), growing up would do it. Abandonment by the BFF (Best Friend Forever) for the new girl in third grade; the sheer meanness of middle school; cancelled out for Friday night because of a better offer from a guy.

Somewhere in the busyness of raising kids, she began to appear to me. I am sure I didn't name her at first. Raised with a patriarchal God, I was not prepared to meet the face of God at the Mothers-of-Preschoolers meeting, any more than those now grown-up preschoolers are today. I might not have recognized her in the soulful conversation that decades later still leaves unfinished sentences demanding more.

She continues to march into my world with joy and passion...

She has walked into my life and we have *known* each other in small groups across the world.

I have met her in powerful written words that explained my life in ways I didn't know I needed until I wondered how she got inside my brain and my life and described it all perfectly.

And lest I think she might have belonged exclusively to the beginning and middle of life, she continues to march into my world with joy and passion, demanding that I stop long enough to savor the bonds of soul sisters...renewed, begun...in what may be the richest season of all.

The face of God in soul sisters—a gift I want to lavish on my daughters and granddaughters, for they, too, wear her face—knowing full well that the recognition, the savoring of sister-love—is an individual awakening. Seeping into the marrow so conclusively, it leaves me startled that I could have ever missed its foundational role in my life.

UNTIL THE BLESSING COMES
MARGARET ROSE

It is Advent again, season of waiting and anticipation. I wonder this year if it is real. What are we waiting for? Is it, as some say, watching for the light? That is real for us Northerners in December. Is it peace? Hard to imagine that this year, with two wars, Haiti in ruins, tribal fighting, the Mideast in turmoil, terrorist threats. Considering this, can I still hold to that Advent hope that this is the year peace really will break out?

Can we hold on until the blessing comes?

My own life is abundant, yet lacking while so many are suffering. I recently saw a YouTube video of GLBT folks who assure us that, "It gets better." For them, maybe. But what about the recent United Nations vote which allowed being gay as an acceptable reason for countries to have the death penalty? Or the woman sentenced to death for blasphemy, or the couple murdered for marrying across religious lines?

My mother would say, "It was ever thus." So take heart and keep on keeping on. Our work is that of the persistent widow whose request Jesus finally grants because she is wearing him out with her persistence. It is like Jacob wrestling with the angel and saying, "I will not let go until you bless me." Yet I wonder, is the work really making a difference, enabling good? Is it worth it? Can we hold on until the blessing comes?

My cat gives me the answer. She persists in trying to sit in my lap, insistent in her crawling, searching for a new way to get in—right, left, under legs, over shoulder. I gently push, then shove her, over and over. She finally settles herself at my head, just under a warm light, but only to bide her time for another pounce. Is that hope? Anticipation? Advent waiting? Well, maybe cats don't have it exactly. But she certainly acts "as if" and with full expectation of success each time. She does not give up. Neither should we.

MIDNIGHT ORISON
JOY NIMNOM KRAUS

With gratitude I sink each night.
God is the air to which I speak
with faith that goes beyond a faith
in things unseen. Yet, to lie down
in comfort with no thanks seems void
of heart, as if the riches were
of my own doing. True, I guard them well.

But mine is finite power. The world
is rife with chance to strip us of good fortune.
Tenuous is my hold on what I love.
And in the thanks there is an unsaid plea,
that what I do not bank on will come through
for me, will sweep aside my questioning
and blanket me so surely that I'll sleep secure.

. . . .

WHEN OUR POWERS WANE
NANCY R. DUVALL

O Lord of snow and sleet,
O Lord of sun and rain,
we thank thee that we have meat
    to eat, friends to greet, promises to keep.
And when our earthly powers wane,
Lord give us grace to praise thy name.

Author Biographies

Anonymous

To my brother 94

Anonymous

Love 64
Faith and healing 70
Hope and redemption 100

Anonymous

Heartbroken 82
Ribs cracked, nose broken 83

Devon Anderson

Swedish coffee and a young saint 102

Devon Anderson is a priest in the Diocese of Minnesota. As Executive Director of Episcopalians for Global Reconciliation, she works with dioceses to better connect their belief with measurable, effective action in mission.

Noël Alhbum Bailey

Unexpected blessings 103

Noël Bailey has worked in Episcopal parishes most of her adult life. She is currently serving at St. Paul's in Lancaster, New Hampshire, and rejoices in God's grace and constant surprises.

Judith Holloway Baum

Between us 52
The real *world* 69
A mystic's polar bear 110

Judith Holloway Baum received her B.A. degree in philosophy from Agnes Scott College in Georgia and is certified by the Shalem Institute for Spiritual Formation in the leading of contemplative prayer for groups and retreats. She lives in North Little Rock, Arkansas.

Angela Boatright-Spencer

Reconciliation 44
Redemption and grace 84

A former journalist and nun, Angela Boatright-Spencer is now an Episcopal priest of twenty years, a published author, a happy mother of sons, and a delighted wife. Based in Charlotte, North Carolina, she is author of *In the Time of Trouble* and co-author with her husband Richard of *The Heir* and *The Molasses Tree.*

Sally M. Brower

Dishing up holy food and drink 60
A mother's hope 88
The love child of Holy Mother
        Wisdom 114

A priest at St. Martin's Episcopal Church in Charlotte, North Carolina, Sally Brower expresses her devotion to God in art and makes meaning of holy encounter through her ministries of preaching, spiritual direction, and leading retreats.

Elizabeth Buening

Blame 72
Fine 98

Elizabeth Buening, a creative director at a major television network, lives in New York City and finds joy in the small moments of life as well as in photography, dance class, and on the soccer field. She has developed stories and friendships with Wild Angels and other writing groups. She is also a certified Rape Crisis & Domestic Violence Counselor and Volunteer Advocate with the St. Luke-Roosevelt Crime Victims Treatment Center, www.cvtc-slr.org/.

Cynthia Caruso

To fail or not to fail 22
My first granddaughter isn't 46
Radiant light 59

Cynthia Caruso, a math teacher, lived the first half of her life in northern California, and most of the second half in Comfort, Texas. In 2006 she moved to Vermont, and in 2009 to Zuni, New Mexico. She is now a student at Seminary of the Southwest in Austin, Texas.

Wanda Ruth Copeland

A priest in the Diocese of Minnesota since 1994, Wanda Ruth Copeland was married to Tom Johnson for twenty-four years. In 2009, Tom was diagnosed with acute mylogenous leukemia, which caused his death thirteen months later. Wanda is now learning to live on her new path.

Barbara Cawthorne Crafton

Barbara Cawthorne Crafton is an Episcopal priest and author. She heads The Geranium Farm, www.geraniumfarm.org, an institute for the encouragement of spiritual growth and practice. The Farm publishes her Almost-Daily eMos, read by thousands worldwide.

Nancy R. Duvall

Nancy R. Duvall is the wife of retired Bishop Charles F. Duvall, mother of three children, and grandmother of six. She loves to garden, walks with a friend every morning, and serves on a board to help the abandoned children of Moldova. The Duvalls live in Columbia, South Carolina.

Lynn Fairfield

Retired from college teaching, Lynn Fairfield moved back to Massachusetts where she joined the world's highest concentration of sixty-something, book-loving, slightly eccentric women. She is a grateful member of an Episcopal church with a woman rector.

Lindsay Hardin Freeman

The editor of this book, Lindsay Hardin Freeman is a priest of twenty-five years. She is the author of *The Scarlet Cord: Conversations with God's Chosen Women*, (www.scarletcordbook.com), *The Best of Vestry Papers*, and, with her husband Leonard, co-author of *Good Lord, Deliver Us: A Lenten Journey*. A ten-year survivor of breast cancer, Lindsay remains grateful to Christ for healing, life, and companionship. The Freemans live in Orono, Minnesota.

Janet F. Fuller

Janet F. Fuller, a Southern Baptist pastor for many years, was ordained into the Episcopal priesthood in 2010. She serves as chaplain at Hollins University, Roanoke, Virginia. She is a parent, a poet, and an expert in loss and grief from personal and professional perspectives.

Cathy H. George

Cathy H. George serves as priest-in-charge of the refounding of St. Mary's Episcopal Church in Dorchester, Massachusetts. For twelve years she served as rector of St. Anne's-in-the-Fields Church in Lincoln. She draws inspiration from the natural world, the teachings of Jesus, poetry, her husband, and two grown children.

Coralie Voce Hambleton

Coralie Voce Hambleton is a vocational deacon at St. Paul's Episcopal Church in Marquette, Michigan, and a social worker. A mother, daughter, grandmother, and wife, she is also an avid quilter who experiences God's presence most intensely when he's sitting in the rocking chair of her sewing room or walking with her along the shores of Lake Superior.

Camille Hegg

Camille Hegg has nourished a lifelong love and curiosity of the power of words through writing, preaching, storytelling, and listening to others as they find words to tell the stories of their lives. Camille was ordained in 1978 and has served as a priest in Alabama and Georgia. She lives in Waleska, Georgia, near Atlanta.

Helen L. Hoover

An active Episcopal laywoman, Helen Hoover enjoys sewing, knitting, reading, and traveling. She and her husband are members of Sowers, an RV ministry for Christian retirees.

Nancy Hopkins-Greene

An Episcopal priest and assistant editor at Forward Movement, Nancy Hopkins-Greene also works part-time at the Church of the Redeemer, in Cincinnati, Ohio. More informally, she is the "often-stressed-out parent of two teenagers, a clergy wife, a slow runner, a wanna-be-if-I-had-more-time quilter, composter, and amateur gardener."

Joy Hunter

Joy Hunter is an often busy wife, mom, and working woman who loves those moments when she can sit at Jesus' feet. She is the director of communications for the Episcopal Diocese of South Carolina.

Noël Julnes-Dehner

Poet and author, Noël Julnes-Dehner is an assistant editor at Forward Movement, a priest of thirty-four years, and the writer/producer of *Under Fire: Soviet Women Combat Veterans, WWII*, a widely seen documentary. A resident of Cincinnati, Ohio, she and her husband Joe are developing reading camps for inner-city students.

Ruth Lawson Kirk

Ordained as an Episcopal priest for twenty years, Ruth Lawson Kirk is daily energized by the joy of faith expressed in the congregations she has served, in the heritage of family, and in the companions of her many pilgrimages. She is rector of Christ Church Christiana Hundred in Wilmington Delaware.

Anne Kitch

Anne Kitch awakens early to find solace in Ignatian spirituality and a cup of tea, preparing herself to meet God in the chaos of daily life with two adolescent girls, her husband of twenty-some years, and an active ministry as the Canon for Christian Formation in the Diocese of Bethlehem, in Pennsylvania.

Joy Nimnom Kraus

Joy Nimnom Kraus is a native and current resident of Washington, D.C., and was educated in the D.C. Public Schools. She graduated from George Washington University with a degree in English Literature. Encouraged by her fourth grade teacher, she began writing poetry and continues to do so at age 81.

Florence Krejci

In the suburbs of Los Angeles, Florence Krejci works at being a Wise Older Woman (WOW)

—a child of God, writer, wife, mother, grandmother, and an evergreen Girl Scout. She is a founding member of The Episcopal Community, an emerging, national, nonmonastic order for Episcopal women. See www.theepiscopalcommunity.org

Lee Krug

Lee Krug is a licensed professional counselor and marriage and family therapist. She is married to an Episcopal priest, and they have four children and nine grandchildren. As a member of Christ Church, Hackensack, New Jersey, she is a frequent preacher. Along with writing, she has a special interest in theater and is addicted to Russian literature, art, music, and drama.

Tara Lyle

Tara Lyle, inmate #L7222, is serving her sentence in the Central Mississippi Correctional Facility in Pearl, Mississippi. She has completed a correspondence paralegal course, started a Bible-based study group in her housing unit, and tutored for six years in the prison's vocational school. Most important, she says, her faith in God has been restored.

Erin Martineau

Erin Martineau is a Resident Companion to the Community of the Holy Spirit and shares in the Community's work of Bluestone Farm and Living Arts Center in Brewster, New York. After having spent some time in academia, she is learning to farm and to meditate, and keeps a journal of her reflections on her blog: *One Wild and Precious Life*, found at www.emartineau.com.

Westina Matthews

After working on Wall Street for over two decades, Westina Matthews is an adjunct professor at General Theological Seminary. She is an inspirational speaker, retreat leader, and spiritual director whose practice reflects contemplative living through "holy listening." The author of three books in the *Have A Little Faith* series, she is a contributor to Forward Movement's publications and *Sacred Journey: The Journal of Fellowship and Prayer.*

Carol McCrea

Newly wed after seven years of widowhood and a new member of St. Paul's Church, Morris Plains, Carol McCrea practices as a clinical psychologist in Warren Township, New Jersey.

Kay Collier McLaughlin

Kay Collier McLaughlin is the Deputy for Leadership Development, Transition Ministries, and Communications in the Episcopal Diocese of Lexington. She designed and facilitated the Circles of Power Women's Leadership Program at the University of Kentucky.

Sarah Bryan Miller

Sarah Bryan Miller is a licensed preacher, eucharistic minister, and lector at St. Peter's

Episcopal Church in St. Louis, Missouri. A musician whose first career was singing opera professionally, she is the classical music critic for the *St. Louis Post-Dispatch* and has written meditations for *Forward Day by Day*.

Sara D. Pines

Working it out 29

A member of St. Mark's Episcopal Church in Palatka, Florida, and a Daughter of the King, Sara Pines writes, paints, and enjoys her grandchildren and great-grandchildren.

Margaret Rose

Women making peace 30
Lost coin 63
Witness 109
Until the blessing comes 122

Margaret Rose is Co-Director of Mission for the Episcopal Church. She was previously Director of Women's Ministries at the Episcopal Church Center in New York City, served several urban parishes in Massachusetts, and as rector of St. Dunstan's in Atlanta, Georgia. She recently completed two Olympic distance triathlons, including the New York Triathlon, where she discovered that "one can swim in the Hudson River and live to tell the tale."

Bitsy Ayres Rubsamen

The cross of Christ 58
Come, Lord Christ 107

A member of Christ Church, San Antonio, Texas, Bitsy Ayres Rubsamen is an active prayer minister, spiritual director, and an author of three books that tell the story of her walk with the Lord. Every morning, no matter where she is, she spends closeted time with her Lord, her journal, and her Bible.

Rosemary Radford Ruether

Earthday prayers and exorcisms 78

Rosemary Radford Ruether is the Carpenter Emerita Professor of Feminist Theology at Pacific School of Religion and the Graduate Theological Union in Berkeley, California, as well as the Georgia Harkness Emerita Professor of Applied Theology at Garrett Evangelical Theological Seminary in Evanston, Illinois. A scholar, teacher, and activist in the Roman Catholic Church, she has enjoyed a long and distinguished career and is well known as a groundbreaking figure in Christian feminist theology.

Lauren R. Stanley

Whistling 26
Glass ceiling 28
Flirting 34

Lauren R. Stanley is an Episcopal priest of the Diocese of Virginia who serves as a preacher, celebrant, retreat leader, and consultant. A journalist prior to ordination, she also writes a national newspaper column about God's presence in people's lives. She was a missionary for five years, most recently in Haiti, the largest diocese in the Episcopal Church. From 2005 to 2009 she served as the Episcopal Church's only full-time missionary in Sudan.

Linda Wallenfang

Living with illness 65

A member of St. Anne's Episcopal Church in Green Bay, Wisconsin, Linda Wallenfang believes her mission in life is to share with other women what she has learned through her life challenges. She is president of the Diocese of Fond du Lac's Women's Ministries and Episcopal Church Women, and an avid Green Bay Packers fan.

Anne O. Weatherholt

Folding clothes 25
"He knows who his mother is" 38
Stains on my alb 54

Anne Weatherholt is the rector of St. Mark's Episcopal Church, Lappans, in western Maryland. Her husband, Allan, is also a priest, and they have two grown children. The author of *Breaking the Silence: The Church Responds to Domestic Violence*, she is a State Police chaplain and weekly columnist for the *Herald Mail* of Hagerstown, Maryland.